Books should be returned on or before the
last date stamped below   *20*

16 IAN 2013   2 ... APR 2014   ‾3 NOV 2010
                        ' 2014   ‾7 FE 11
    OCT 05   ‾ JUN 2008
    06   21 JUN 2008   15 JUN 2011
06. JAN 06.
21. JN   05. MAY 09   06. SEP 11
06. MAR 08.   2 9 JUN 2012
                 ‾ 3 SEP 2012 1 2 DEC 2012

Willie's War
&
Other Stories

Willie Smith

The Shetland Times Ltd.
Lerwick
2004

Willie's War & Other Stories

ISBN 1 898852 97 9

First published by The Shetland Times Ltd., 2004.

Front cover photos:
Top left: Willie and Gnr. Jack Thomas, 1940.
Top right: The Shetland Bus Memorial, Main Street, Scalloway,
overlooks the harbour which was home and refuge for the
Norwegian boats during the dark days of world war two. This memorial
was erected by the Shetland Bus Friendship Society in 2003.
The model is of *Andholmen*, one of the Shetland Bus boats.
Bottom: Gordon Highlanders (from left): Willie Hughson,
Attie Williamson, George Horne, Davie Slater,
Andrew Williamson and John Smith.

Back cover photo

Smith, Willie, 1   r, Kenna.

Willie's war &
other stories /
Willie Smith

B SMI

1553291

British Library Cataloguing-in-Publication Data
A catalogue record for this book is available from the British Library.

Printed and published by
The Shetland Times Ltd.,
Gremista, Lerwick,
Shetland ZE1 0PX, UK.

I would like to dedicate this book to the Servicemen and women, British and Norwegian, who were stationed in Shetland during the Second World War, and to the people of Scalloway who lived through those years.

ACKNOWLEDGEMENTS

I am indebted to my son William C. T. Smith, BSc., for the time he has spent correcting my English. My thanks also to three friends with whom I have yarned over the years, Andy Irvine of Asta, John George Nicolson of St. Clair, and Jim Smith, M.B.E., of Berry. Thanks also to Nell Duncan, Georgie Duthie, Eva Smith, Lexie Watt, Stella Sutherland, Nina Slater, Mona Jamieson, Sammy Christie and Harry Cole.

For photos I have to thank: Marina Gray, John G. Nicolson, Mamie Williamson, Nina Slater, Elaine Waddell, Mona Jamieson, Georgie Duthie, Karen Anderson, Keith Pottinger, William C. T. Smith and Vera Smith.

Most of the photos in this book were taken by Clement J. Williamson.

CONTENTS

WILLIE'S WAR

Peace in our time. Those were the Prime Minister's words as he stepped from a plane waving a scrap of paper. Pictures were in all the newspapers, everybody breathed a sigh of relief and went about their business.

However, the clouds of war were never far away and soon we heard Prime Minister Chamberlain was to make an announcement.

"I now inform you that a state of war exists between Great Britain and Germany." I heard Prime Minister Neville Chamberlain's quavering words as a ten-year-old, gathered with family, friends and neighbours round a wireless set on Sunday, 3rd September, 1939. There was much talk of what might happen and it was with feelings of apprehension that we went to bed that night with thoughts of German planes flying overhead and dropping bombs on Shetland. Many people had bad dreams that night.

War meant that windows had to be blacked out and before we got proper black outs I remember a warden coming to our door saying, "I see a chink of light at your window." Eventually we got proper screens so that no light could be seen by the German planes we expected would soon be flying all round us.

We heard one day that a German plane had dropped a bomb on the North Mainland and had killed a rabbit. It was a great story. It was told on the wireless and gave rise to a song which became very popular and was sung by everyone. It was called "Run Rabbit Run".

Bertie Burgess at bomb crater, Vatster, 1939.
© *C.J.W.*

We all had to go to the public hall one day, where we were fitted with gas masks and told to carry them everywhere we went. Then we

Jamsie Williamson and son, Wilfie, 1930s.   © C.J.W.

Gordon Highlanders, 1940.
Courtesy of Mamie Williamson

were given identity cards to carry. Next, ration books, and as there were four in our household, Chrissie, Phyllis, Anna and myself, we registered two with Nicolson & Co., West Shore and two with James Williamson, Merchant, Blacksness.

Six local lads were in the Territorial Army. Willie Hughson, Johnnie Smith, Attie Williamson, Sonny Williamson, Davie Slater and George Horne were called up at the outbreak of war and joined the Gordon Highlanders. Others were called up outwith Scalloway but I'm not sure of their names. Johnnie Smith and Davie Slater were captured at St Valery and for five years were in different prisoner of war camps. They never saw each other again until they were back home in Scalloway. The others were in different theatres of war.

Shetland Gordon Highlanders Reunion in the 1950s, Royal Hotel, Scalloway.

© C.J.W.

Adie's Station

Adie's Station at West Shore was a great playground. Many years ago, in the days of fishing with sail boats, Adies of Voe had reclaimed a large part of the foreshore for a fishing station, with buildings and a long wooden pier. It was here that my cousin, John Umphray, and I played. There were always boats and old cars there. We took them over and had many pretend sea voyages and long car runs. A large piece of tin below a taft, when pounded by two small feet sounded like a fine engine. When we got fed up with boats there were the cars to go for pretend motor tours in.

The car I remember best was a two seater. It was a roadster type, had a wooden steering wheel, leather seats, lots of dials on the dash and a dickie seat at the back. The name of the car escapes me but it belonged to Bob Moore. It was a real classic car and would be much sought after today. No one chased us away from either the boats or cars unless we made too much of a carry on, which was not often. We never vandalised anything. We were always told to respect other people's property, and we did. Failure to do so brought swift action, a clip on the ear, which learned us not to try that again.

Mister Moore

One day a load of sand appeared and we made sandcastles, dug holes and had great fun. Suddenly old Mr Moore arrived, not very tall but a formidable figure of a man. We thought he was going to chase us but he said, "Do you like to dig in the sand boys?" "Oh yes," we said. "Right," he said, "come with me." So we followed him across the Lords Well beach to the smiddy.

In a corner was a pile of small hessian sacks. He pointed and said, "Take as many as you can carry and come back to the sand." Back at the sand Mr Moore said, "Fill the sacks with sand, tie the string at the mouth, lay them along the wall, and at tea time I'll give you a shilling".

Mr Moore, 1938. © C.J.W.

"What are they for Mr Moore?" we wanted to know. "They are going to be built outside doors to protect them from bomb blast," was the reply. We filled the bags and got paid and thought it was great.

West Shore air raid shelter, 2003. © W.S.

Air Raid Shelters

German planes could be seen and heard in the skies above Shetland, and at Scalloway we all expected bombs to come raining down. Three air raid shelters were built in the west shore area of Scalloway. One was at the back of Nicolson's shop, another in the Bungalow garden and the third in the garden at Oregon Cottage. Who authorised them and who paid for them I do not know. Then when the public hall was converted into a military hospital, a shelter was built in the park opposite.

Fortunately, for the people of Scalloway, none of the air raid shelters were ever used for the purpose for which they were built. They can all still be seen today, with two of them in daily use for storage.

Bungalow, West Shore, air raid shelter, 2003.
© W.S.

Air raid shelter, Oregon Cottage, 2003.
© W.S.

Military Hospital air raid shelter, 2003.   © W.T.C.S.

First of Da Sodgers

Soldiers soon arrived in the village and on Ward Hill (Da Wart), West shore they built a small felly hut. A wire on posts ran all the way up to the hut and inside was a phone. One soldier wandered around looking out over the isles for Germans and another sat by the phone. We used to sit in the hut with them and were given the phone to hold. What we expected to hear I do not know.

A short time later they got a sectional hut built on the seaward side of the hill. It had a little stove for warmth and two years ago I noticed a piece of it still lying at the site. At the war's end the hut was dismantled and the sections sledged downhill towards Robbie Rolly. Willie Hutchison and myself, not long started work, did the job. Robbie Rolly was a landmark on the road to Port Arthur. I recall seeing a photo or painting showing a natural arch, which was destroyed when a road was built to serve the new fishing station called Port Arthur. Who Robbie Rolly was I don't know. During the war this was where the guard hut for the Royal Artillery battery was situated, and was as far as we bairns were allowed.

Two tents appeared on Adie's Station one day. One was bell shaped and had four-foot high sides. The other was the shape you expect tents to be. Little boys would have to investigate.

Finding an opening in the bell tent, two little heads peeped in. Inside were four beds, a trestle table and a form to sit on. On the table was a Singer sewing machine and seated on the form was a soldier. While turning the handle of the sewing machine and pushing an article of clothing under the flashing needle, he gave us a cheery greeting. "Come away in boys, come away in."

He was a tailor and repaired and altered uniforms. The other three soldiers did guard duty at Port Arthur where the gun battery was being built. The tailor, his name was Peter, asked if any one of us could turn the machine handle. When he said stop, you had to stop on the instant. We visited him after school and had great fun turning the handle. We never found out what was in the other tent. Then one Monday morning both tents had disappeared. That was the way of the military and we never saw the tailor again.

The Refugee Boat

One day some of us boys were playing at West Shore when we heard the familiar tonk tonk of a Swedish or Norwegian boat's engine. It was an interesting time for young folk, and we liked to know what was going on, so we hastened to the shoreline to see this craft. It had the familiar look of a Norwegian boat and it was slowly heading for Blacksness Pier. The year was either 1940 or 1941, so sensing something strange we headed for Blacksness at top speed.

At that time a lot of people stayed in the Blacksness area. There were 11 folk in Blacksness House and three next door in the Post Office. At the top of the brae and in Jamsie Williamson's shop were another five people. Johnson's Court area housed ten, and along the New Street were another 18.

By the time the boat was approaching the west side of the pier a lot of people had gathered, including us bairns. Suddenly an army car arrived in a hurry and out jumped an officer and a sergeant. Then an open-backed lorry appeared with a lot of armed soldiers. They all jumped off and the sergeant positioned them where the boat was going to berth. The villagers and bairns surged forward as men, women and children could be seen on the deck of the boat. These were the first obvious refugees we had seen and we did not want to miss anything. At this intrusion the officer turned and made shooing gestures with his arms, like someone chasing hens out of a cornfield. "Everyone off the quay," he shouted. We fell back a few paces, but not too far, so he continued to flap his arms for us to back off a bit further.

Gently the boat nudged alongside the pier and three soldiers scrambled aboard. They herded most of the men, the women and young children ashore and onto the back of the lorry. One of the soldiers handed three rockets up to them, like the ones we set off in a bottle on bonfire night. Some villager wondered who would see the rockets if the lorry was attacked by German planes at the Brig of Fitch. What became of these Norwegians we never heard and I have no memories of the boats name or what happened to it.

The Road Block

At the foot of the Mill Brae a road block was built and manned by soldiers twenty four hours a day. It consisted of three huge blocks of concrete. Two were on the upper side of the road, and the third halfway between, but on the seaward side of the road. Thus they formed a triangle.

Road block, 2003.   © W.T.C.S.

Road block, 2003.   © W.T.C.S.

The two ends of a thick wire rope were buried in the concrete blocks on the upper side of the road, and the middle of the rope was looped into a slot on the seaward block. The wire had to be unhooked in order to let vehicles past. This was not, I would have thought, an easy job to do, especially with a vehicle moving towards you at speed.

As if this was not enough, there were two great barrel shaped rounds of concrete which were to be rolled in place between the wire. No car or lorry would have got past that lot, so I suppose

Road block, 2003. © *W.T.C.S.*

in Scalloway we were safe from a road based attack. I can remember being in the area many times but do not recall ever seeing the wire or concrete rounds in place.

After the war the concrete blocks and rounds of concrete were just rolled and pushed into the East Voe where they still lie and can be seen to this day.

Nicolson's House

By this time there were many soldiers in Scalloway. Men from the Pioneer Corps were billeted in the Net Loft (later to become Norway House) at West Shore for a while. After them came the Royal Artillery boys until their camp at Port Arthur gun battery was ready. Conditions were primitive and there was no heating. They had a corrugated iron shed with toilets and washing facilities.

I stayed in the first floor of Nicolson's House, less than one hundred yards from the Net Loft, with my older sisters, Chrissie, Phyllis and Anna. In the west end rooms on the ground floor were Basil and Daisy Grant, with their two daughters, Sheila and Mona.

One fine day Daisy set little Mona out in her pram. Some time later Basil arrived home, and as they only had two rooms asked where Mona was. Daisy answered, "Sitting in her pram." His reply was that the pram was empty.

Norway House, West Shore, 2003.   © W.S.

Mona and Sheila, 1940s.   © C.J.W.
Courtesy of Mona Jamieson

Daisy went up the road questioning the neighbours and Basil rushed down to the water's edge and the Pier. Where was Mona?

Two passing Norwegians, who often visited the Grants, had lifted Mona from her pram and she was now sitting quite contentedly in Norway House, eating chocolate. Inga Roald, who worked in Norway House, learned Mona to walk. She would prop her along a wall, step back, hold out her hands and say, "Er du gonna go nu Mona?" (that's how it sounded), and Mona would walk.

Mona has a wooden cup brought from occupied Norway and Sheila has a wooden puppet made by one of the Norwegians, and still working after all these years. Mona also has a lamp made by one of the Norwegian engineers from a brass shell case. This was gifted to Basil and Daisy. One of the Norwegians called Hans Bakland carried a photo of Mona and Sheila all through the Shetland Bus operations and a few years ago presented the photo to Mona.

In the east end rooms was Agnes Elizabeth Thomson, originally from Bigton and better known as Aggie Leebie. She walked with the help of a crutch and always wore a moorit wool shawl, or as we called it, a "hap".

Like lots of other houses, both doors were open to men from the Pioneer Corps, the Artillery and the Norwegians, in fact anyone who wanted to sit by the fire and get warmed up, as well as have a cup of tea and a chat. A Norwegian called Harold was a great comic and kept everyone laughing, more so if he had a little dram. Some nights with the

Aggie Leebie, 1920s.
Courtesy of Georgie Duthie

sounds of merriment coming from Aggie's one would have wondered if there was really a war on.

Aggie's rooms had a Number Seven stove and it could give out some heat, so in the dark days of winter she always had visitors. Sometimes Norwegians back from a trip to Norway, tired and exhausted, would visit Aggie and with the heat from the stove would fall asleep, some lying on the sofa and some on her bed. One of the Pioneers in fact felt so at home in Aggie's that he wrote a piece of poetry.

AGGIE'S CANTEEN

Far away to the north in the Shetlands
Within sight and sound of the sea,
There, a house which for me holds sweet memories
A haven on earth 'twas for me.

It was owned by a kind hearted lady
The finest that ever was seen,
And to show just how it meant to us
We christened it Aggie's Canteen.

Now Aggie is not any flapper,
She has lived, aye, full many a year
But we cared not if she had been ninety,
She filled the place of one we hold dear.

And though I shall never return there
The memory will always be green,
Of the times, when sad and downhearted.
I found solace in "Aggies Canteen".

Sig. Ben Clark. 196 Coy. Pioneer Corps.

Courtesy of Georgie Duthie

Even before the war Aggie's was a gathering place, always lots of yarns going. As bairns we were always in and out of Aggie's as well. Aggie died on April 7th, 1949 at the age of 67 years.

Da Sodgers

A camp was being built at Berry and the new houses at Houl Road and Meadowfield Road were taken over by the military. There were lots of different regiments in Scalloway. The Military Police were also in the village, very smart they were with their red caps and highly polished boots, and batons hanging from their belts. We always viewed the Red Caps from a distance. They kept order among the troops. I never heard of any trouble, or if there was we never heard of it.

I remember us boys talking to some of the Royal Artillery soldiers one night and one kept saying, "cor blimey". Soon we were saying cor

Meadowfield Road.   *© C.J.W.*

blimey at everything that happened. Some of the older folk were not sure if this was a new swear word we had picked up from da sodgers.

We got to know a lot of the artillery men and some used to visit our home. We had a wireless set, not very common in those days, and one night when the news was on we discovered three artillery men standing outside listening. They were duly invited in to listen, given a cup of tea, and told to come again, which they did, and often brought others with them. L/cpl Jack Thomas, transferred from the 4th Gloucester Regt., Gnr. Ernie Mathers, Gnr George Haynes, Gnr Ronald West and Bdr. Eddie Plant were just a few I remember. Jack Thomas was not a very big man but a lovely singer. In our house he sang Welsh songs and hymns.

Andrew Johnson, of Kirk Park, had

Willie and Gnr. Jack Thomas, 1940. *© C.J.W.*

James W. Duncan, Gerald Duncan and Bill Mouatt sitting on gun barrel, 1945.
Courtesy of Georgie Duthie

some dairy cattle and was a supplier of milk to quite a lot of West Shore folk. In the summer time the cattle were grazed at the East Park and were brought home for milking and kept in the byre overnight. Andrew's wife, Katrine, sold the milk from a small dairy. It and the byres were at the back of Adies House, at the face of Adie's quarry.

One morning they could not understand why one of the cows gave no milk. Next day it was the same, and the next. It seemed that someone might be milking the cows so they decided to put on a watch. Very early in the morning, from a nearby shed, a watch was on. A Royal Artillery soldier with a bucket in his hand was seen going into the byre. They gave him a few minutes then crept quietly in and there he was (caught teat in hand) milking a cow. Apparently he was used to farm work, and knew that milk was good for you.

When the battery was fully operational, they had two four-inch guns, a rapid fire Howitzer, the usual machine guns and a searchlight. The guns had to be fired to see how they worked so word was sent round the village to expect big bangs at a set time, and they were big bangs.

Sometimes they would practice at night. We used to have the window wide open and could see the whole village in the light from the explosions. The poor old Green Holm suffered from these practice shots. Looking from Blacksness, when they fired the Howitzer, you could see Black Skerry being blasted to pieces. It was exciting times for youngsters, but worrying times for our elders.

An artillery man called Freddie, who visited Willie Fullerton's house, returned to Shetland many times after the war. Georgie Duthie said that on one occasion Freddie told some boys at Port Arthur that he was in Scalloway when the big guns were here in the wartime. "Well," they asked, "if it was a war who did you fight." Freddie just laughed.

Ernie Mathers wrote in a book, "You have made me welcome to your home, may God bless you all. Peace be with you." I'm sure these words expressed what a lot of sodger boys felt. I had got a lapel badge from one of the R.A.s and was showing it off one night in our house to Staff Sergeant Rattery of the R.A.M.C. "I have a lot of badges home," he announced. "When I go on leave next I will take them back to you."

Two or three weeks later he was off on leave. Would he remember

Ernie Mather's writing.

I wondered? On his return he visited us that same evening. He stood for a while with his great coat on and told us about his journey. I, of course, did not dare ask about badges, but was now thinking he had forgot. Then he took off his coat, and there round his waist was a belt full of badges. I clapped my hands and danced in front of him. To say I was excited would be an understatement.

One Sunday afternoon in 1941 I was with some boys outside the post office at Blacksness when we heard a very loud bang. An explosion in wartime was to be expected. We looked at one another then all ran to the west side of the Blacksness sheds. Looking towards Burra Isle we saw a great pall of black smoke rising in the air. Later we heard a mine had exploded and killed two men.

My sisters, like other Shetland women, knitted. George Haynes ordered two pairs of Fair Isle gloves to be ready as soon as possible as he would soon be going on leave. One day I was told to go to the battery with a verbal message for George to say the gloves were ready. The camp gates were at Robbie Rolly and the guard asked what I wanted. When I said I had a message for Gnr George Haynes he directed me to a Nissen hut. It was covered all over with concrete and inside was the generating plant. I remember the noise the engine made and trying to shout above the noise. Message delivered I would liked to have had a look round, maybe even seen the big guns, but that was not allowed, so it was back out through the barbed wire gate at Rolly.

Port Arthur pier was where the harbour examination boat lay. I remember two boats being stationed there, first the *Aliped*, and then the *Fear Not*. The skipper of the former was Alfred Coull, a man from Wick. He, his wife and daughter Jessie, stayed in a little house at West Shore. The skipper of the *Fear Not* was Jamsie Christie from Burra Isle. When a boat was approaching the harbour an officer from the Battery would set out on the examination boat to look at her papers. As the examination boats operated more or less outside the harbour area we hardly ever saw them. The only time I saw the *Fear Not* in action was to help haul a drunk man from the mid harbour. He had fallen from Ertie Inkster's packet boat and was saved from drowning by some Trondra people rowing very fast from Blacksness pier, before being hauled aboard the *Fear Not*.

A few names of regiments come to mind: Seaforth Highlanders, Gordon Highlanders, Cameronians, Highland Light Infantry, Kings

Captain and crew of Fear Not.   © *C.J.W.*

Some of the Shetland Home Defence men, 1942.   © *C.J.W.*

Home Defence men: Lowrie Moar, Johnie Nicolson, Alex Hughson and Sammy Sutherland, 1942. ©C.J.W.

Own Scottish Borderers, Black Watch, Royal Engineers, Royal Army Service Corps, Royal Army Ordnance Corps, Royal Army Medical Corps, Royal Berkshire Regiment, Pioneer Corps, and of course the Royal Artillery (not, I should add, all in the village at the same time.) There may have been others that I don't remember.

There was also the Shetland Home Defence, a fine bunch of men who came from all over Shetland and did guard duty wherever they were needed. A platoon of them, North Isles men, did guard duty in gun posts at Berry farm, overlooking the building of Berry camp. They complained that here they were guarding Sheepy's farm when they would have been better employed at home guarding their own crofts and farms. One wet and cold day, John Smith took them all in the farmhouse and gave them a good dram of whisky, and they all had a good yarn. There were no more grumbles after that.

I remember half a Nissen hut on Blacksness pier where men stayed while doing guard duty at the pier. A Lerwick man, Alex Hughson played reels on the fiddle and a man from Unst, Sammy Sutherland, would dance. We young ones would dance with him, we thought it was great fun. Many years later I met up with Sammy again; I married one of his daughters.

Da Home Guard

We should not forget the Home Guard, a mixture of young and older men. Many older men were called up for service in the Home Guard. Andy Irvine from Asta tells that he was in the Scalloway Home Guard and, "That fine body of men were so good that not one German ever set foot in Scalloway." He was right.

The Home Guard headquarters in Scalloway was in the Bank of Scotland buildings on Main Street, and it was from there that patrols

Scalloway Home Guard when first formed, 1940.   © *C.J.W.*

were allocated and sent out. They had a Nissen hut in front of the Scalloway Hotel, on what we called Burnett's Station, for their stores and equipment. In it was a Bogey stove, and the store keeper, an elderly member, would light it most nights.

Two young lads, Jim Smith and Angus Craig, decided for a joke to stuff a bag in the chimney. That night when the stove was lit the Nissen hut rapidly filled with smoke. The hut was abandoned until the lum was cleared. Later, when things returned to normal, the whole company was paraded and the Major gave them a pep talk and asked for the guilty men to own up. Jim and Angus stepped forward and for punishment had to light the fire every night for some time afterwards.

Sometimes the Home Guard did duty in the hut on top of Ward Hill (Da Wart). One really stormy night two locals were on duty and one of them passed the time writing this poem.

> *Ye slumbers of Scalloway so snugly cuddled in,*
> *Sleep on, for we will guard your homes all*
> *through the storms din;*
> *Sleep on I say, and Magnie too, for we are here*
> *tonight,*
> *No ravaging wolves skulk 'round your doors*
> *while we are on the height.*

*We speak of soldiers of the fray, blood stained
   by many a battle,
But we're more used to humping coal, and
   driving stubborn cattle.
But as they say, the truth will out, and dare I
   shrink to tell;
If "Jerry" landed here tonight, we'd both be off
   like hell.*

John George Nicolson.
Courtesy of John Nicolson

John George Nicolson recalls one Sunday afternoon, a fine day with some frost and patches of ice on the roads. Archie, the Sergeant Major, decided that some of the young lads needed to get more practice with their marching and halting. When they arrived at the chosen venue, Blacksness Pier, they all stood in line to watch Archie demonstrate the correct way to march and halt. Giving the correct commands Archie started to march. On the command to halt, his feet hit a patch of ice and left the ground, and he fell flat on his back. John and the others helped Archie up and got a fish box for him to sit on, and there they stayed for the next hour before going back to HQ on Main Street. The sergeant major was very shaken but otherwise unhurt. There was no more marching and halting that day.

On one occasion, at the firing range near Asta loch, there was almost a riot. An elderly member of the platoon, who was a bit short sighted, lay down on the grass with his 303 rifle to fire at the target which was up on the hillside. Some of the boys reckoned that he never saw the target, but he fired anyway. The bullet sizzled its way through the grass in front of him and buried itself in the peat moor. One of the younger lads said in a loud stage whisper, "Boy, that sure was a daisy cutter." The sergeant had a job to smooth ruffled feathers and treat it all as a joke.

On another occasion Tingwall Home Guard and Scalloway Home

Guard were having a mock battle in or near the castle. It was friendly rivalry with a vengence. When someone said "bang" you were supposed to be declared dead. There was a big argument as to who had won, and who was and was not declared dead. One local gent said most vociferously that he was most certainly not dead. At that, someone at the back of the crowd foolishly fired a shotgun. It was loaded with a blank cartridge but the wad from it struck the vociferous gent between the eyes, and a voice said, "Du is dead noo."

Andy tells of many dugouts and places where the Home Guard used to go on duty. One dugout was in a convenient and handy spot, very close to the Royal Artillery battery and their canteen. If the occasion arose that a message had to be passed to a patrol in a dugout then a messenger was sent, but he had to know the password in use at that particular time. Andy says that if the password was not known then the messenger might have been shot, and that would have been a terrible waste of a bullet, as bullets were not very plentiful in the Home Guard.

One night a message had to be sent to the dug out at Port Arthur. The man picked had a slight stammer, more so in a situation like this. The password was Jasmine. When he approached the dugout he was challenged. "Halt. Who goes there, what is the password?" He tried to say Jasmine, but in the excitement of the moment could not say the word. All that came out was, "Ja, Ja, Ja." At that a slightly inebriated voice came from the dugout, "It's a bloody German, shoot the bugger."

Lots of men joined the Home Guard, some because they had to and others because they wanted to. One who wanted to was Jim Smith from Berry farm. The Home Guard gave one the opportunity to fire guns, and so, in his very early teens he joined up.

There were plenty of guns, Jim said, and one time at the farm he had a Browning automatic rifle, a 300 Ross rifle, a 303 Lee Enfield and a Sten gun; a small armoury.

At the lambing time a crow had been giving a lot of trouble to lambs and pecking at ewes. One Sunday morning Jim saw the crow sitting on a telephone pole at the front of the house. He thought he would get the lad this time and brought out the Sten gun, which had a full magazine. Jim took aim at the crow and pulled the trigger. The gun was set on single shot, but something was wrong. The gun went off on automatic, the crow fled away but the gun kept firing. It would not stop. The whole

Jim Smith, M.B.E.   © *C.J.W.*

magazine went down over Scalloway somewhere but as it was early on a Sunday morning luckily there was no one about. A red faced Jim got back into the house fast and at the next parade had some fancy explaining to do.

Once a ewe was lambing on the hillside just above the football pitch, straight across from the Berry Camp. Jim came out from the house and saw a big black back gull pecking at the newborn lamb. Quickly fetching the 303 rifle, Jim laid the gun across a dyke, took aim at the black back and fired. Like the crow, Jim said, the black back flew away. But what Jim had not seen was the Berry Camp sergeant major, at the camp side of the dyke. When someone fires a 303 rifle over your head it's bound to give you a fright, and the sergeant major was furious. He gave Jim a fearful telling off, which in its turn infuriated Jim, who said he could quite cheerfully have shot the sergeant major, but politely refrained from doing so. Some time later Jim joined the Royal Air Force.

The Smith Gun

The TV programme, Dad's Army, I have been told depicts the Home Guard right down to the finest detail. A field gun bearing the name Smith was brought from Lerwick for an exercise, complete with a high ranking officer who was in charge of the Shetland area. The idea, the officer said, was to get the gun to the top of the Berry hill and overlooking Burwick, where it would bombard the Germans when they landed on the Burwick beach.

The gun had a barrel about five feet long and two and a half inches in diameter. It was mounted on two wheels about four feet in diameter. When the gun was in place it would be tipped over on to its side, resting on one of the wheels, so it could then be swivelled round on the wheel axle. A real primitive weapon, and it was probably a good job it was never fired. Well it could not be, as they had no ammunition for it.

The first step was to get it to the top of the hill, but this was going to be difficult as it was quite heavy. Someone suggested a horse would be best, and the officer said, "Now that is a splendid idea. Would the farm over there have one?" Jim Smith went to their farm and got a horse. They got the gun and horse hitched up with chain traces and a member of the platoon, who was used to working with horses, took charge of the drive to the top of the hill and soon the Smith gun was in position. When the Burwick beach was lined up and the gun ready for firing there were congratulations all round. The splendid exercise was then concluded and the officer declared it a great success.

There was still one thing to do however, get the gun down to the bottom of the hill. This caused the only bit of trouble as with no shafts and just chain traces the gun would run on to the horse and that would not do. The officer wondered what was to be done. A big discussion followed with lots of suggestions but no decisions. Jim Smith, with an air of complete innocence said, "Its on wheels, why not let it go? It will run downhill itself." The officer looked relieved and said, "What a jolly good idea." So gun and horse were unhitched, and the gun let go. The gun ran down hill all right. With gathering speed and bouncing splendidly it ran right into the Berry pond and settled down in the mud. I wonder if the officer's face had the expression you might have seen portrayed by Captain Mainwaring.

The Bunker

Two regular soldiers were with the Scalloway company. Captain Hutchison from the Kings Own Scottish Borderers and Sergeant Knight from the Royal Scots. Home Guard HQ for Shetland, based in Lerwick, decided that an underground unit should be formed with men from all the companies. Their task, not if Shetland was invaded, but when, would be to emerge and blow up the German tanks and cause havoc among the enemy troops.

For the Scalloway group a large Anderson shelter was built underground, in a low area on the hillside northeast from the loch of Njuggles Water. It was constructed by Royal Engineers and men from the Home Guard. On the side of the hill they dug a huge hole, built the Anderson

Arnold Duncan at bunker hatch, 2002.   © W.S.

Inside the bunker, 2002.   © W.S.

shelter into it and then covered all with earth. Andy Irvine says the divots to cover the infilled earth were brought by Bren gun carriers from near the Scord and from Veensgarth. When they were all in place the special unit was well and truly hidden.

John George Nicolson added however, that with the Bren gun carriers making tracks through the heather, all the tracks leading to the well hidden bunker would be seen from the air.

Entry was through a flat hatch, operated by counter weights running over two pipes and opened by a wire hidden some considerable distance away.

Willie in the bunker, 2002.   © A.D.

One Sunday they were to be inspected by a very high ranking officer from British home forces so everything had to be spick and span. The pipes got a good rubbing with grease so the hatch would open and close effortlessly. The grease, of course, would be removed before the visit and the pipes polished just in case anyone wanted to go down.

When the HRO, clad in a beautiful lambs-wool coat, and all his retinue arrived for the inspection, six or eight special unit men with suitably blackened faces, were there with their NCO. After speaking to the men the HRO wanted to go down into the underground chamber for a look. When he emerged everyone could see two dirty great strips on the back of his beautiful lambs-wool coat. Someone had forgot to remove the grease and polish the pipes.

Andy said you could hear breath being sucked in, but nobody said a word. The HRO and his men said their goodbyes and departed over the hill toward their cars. The special unit men waited for what they knew would be coming and come it did. Twenty minutes or so later Captain Hutchison arrived back and gave them the roasting of their lives. The large Anderson shelter is still in place to this day.

One night the army decided to test the special unit men to see how prepared they were. A number of officers would observe, with one acting as an umpire, judging the success or otherwise of the test. The men all gathered and proceeded to the bunker, where they blackened their faces and hands and made ready to deal with the Germans. The bunker was fitted out with bunk beds, tinned food, guns, grenades and all the necessities of life.

John George was sent to the top of the hill to watch for the army officers. He saw a convoy of staff cars and motor bikes coming down the side of Dale. He waited until they were at the burn of Njuggles Water and on their way up the hill. John then ran towards the bunker, gave a report to the umpire and rejoined the special unit.

When the officers were all in position and ready to observe the umpire set off a thunderflash. That was the signal. Up went the hatch and out poured the special unit men armed to the teeth. Each man carried a sten gun, pockets full of ammunition and, in the breast pockets of their tunics, hand grenades. The special unit men were ready to deal with any situation. They had to form in a circle as quickly as they could, so it would appear they were defending all the points of the compass. It all went well and the umpire gave them top marks.

The officers, numbering in the teens, were a very sociable lot. In talking the special unit men discovered they were indeed honoured to be inspected by no less than two generals. One was GOC Scottish Command and the other was GOC Tactical Command. They all congratulated the special unit men and told them how well they were doing. The special unit men however had a different outlook. They would be lucky if they lasted ten minutes against Adolf Hitler's Storm Troops.

The Tank Buster

One Sunday a company of fifteen or so Scalloway Home Guard men went to the firing range near the Sandy Loch at Lerwick. My Uncle Lowrie was the driver and he had a lorry from the firm of James Johnson and Sons, Scalloway. The company was commanded by Lieutenant James Thomson, a Scalloway man and an engineer at Moore's Smiddy. The instructor for the day was a regular army man, Sergeant Hogg, whose mode of transport was an army pick up truck. The only other qualified driver was Jimmy Leask, a workmate of Lieutenant Thomson.

The company had previously practised throwing hand grenades

which had a four second fuse. They had to take a firm hold of the grenade, pull out the pin which held the firing plate mechanism in place, then throw the grenade. When it was thrown the plate, firmly held in the hand, was released and the grenade was primed to explode in four seconds. There were sandbagged areas and conveniently handy peat stacks for cover for throwing from. They had all previously managed this with no problems.

This particular Sunday Sergeant Hogg said they were going to practice with a new type of grenade, a number 68 anti tank contact grenade. It was shaped like an egg timer, with a copper head and a copper cone inside so that the explosive material would take the least line of resistance and go straight in to the tank, if the aim was accurate.

This grenade, he said, had been developed so it could be fired from a discharger cup fitted to an adapted 303 rifle. The operator had to sit down, legs straight out in front, with the rifle on his left side, turned upside down and held at an angle of forty five degrees with the butt on the ground. With the discharger cup on the rifle there were also sights, which stuck out to the side. It was not easy to line up the sights with the target which was a pile of stones and rubbish about a hundred yards distant. The general opinion was that the whole set up was very awkward. It also had to be done in the open as there was no shelter. The rifle used blank cartridges and when firing the operator had to flick the trigger as there was quite a kick back which could quite easily have broken a finger. The grenade had a pin like the other grenades and the operator had to pull the pin before fitting into the discharger cup. When the pin was pulled it revealed a thin brass wire that would break when the grenade was jettisoned from the rifle and so be ready to explode on the target.

Several of the company had fired a grenade and all seemed to be going well. On the right of the operator, about five yards distant, stood Lieutenant James Thomson, or as he was known locally, Jeemsie. On the left, also about five yards distant stood Sergeant Hogg. The rest of the company stood in a semi circle. The next man to fire did not have as good vision as the previous ones and had difficulty aiming. This operator only managed to fire the grenade a short distance. Pieces of the grenade could be heard whistling overhead so Sergeant Hogg immediately put the rest of the company behind the peat stacks to be on the safe side. "Look over the stacks," he said, "and watch what is going on."

The next man to fire was my Uncle Lowrie. He got in the sitting position, legs out in front, rifle at forty five degrees and picked up the grenade. He pulled the pin and dropped the grenade in the discharger, but before he could pull the trigger, WHAM, the grenade exploded in the discharger cup. The three men were enveloped in a cloud of smoke and disappeared from view.

Two of the company, Jimmy Leask and John George Nicolson, standing at the end of a peat stack, were quick off the mark and rushed towards the smoke. The rest of the men hurried behind. Jimmy was just on the edge of the smoke when Lieutenant Thomson came staggering out, blood pouring from his face and running down over his leather jacket. Jimmy just grabbed him before he fell. Jeemsie had a lot of shrapnel in his jaw and had lost some teeth, but his worst wound, which they did not know of at that time, was shrapnel in the groin and he was bleeding profusely. Sergeant Hogg had got a piece of shrapnel close to one eye and for some time after it was feared that he might lose the use of it, but he made a full recovery. Uncle Lowrie was still sitting where he was, both ankles peppered with shrapnel. In a way they were all lucky because the explosion took the line of least resistance and went forward because of the copper cone.

Sergeant Hogg was the driver of the pick up and Lowrie was the driver of the lorry. With them both injured the only other driver was Jimmy Leask. All three injured men were now hurriedly got into the pick up and with some men to support them, Jimmy set off at top speed for the Gilbert Bain Hospital.

This left the others with a box of number 68 anti tank grenades, a lorry and no driver. A very young member of the company, Leonard Anderson, said he was learning to drive and if they were willing to go with him he would take the lorry. As they were all anxious about how Jeemsie, Lowrie and Sergeant Hogg were doing they climbed in. One of the men picked up the box of grenades to set it on the lorry. An older member thought it best to leave them where they were, beside the sandbags, as more of them might be faulty and lorry and men could all be blown to pieces. Leonard drove down the Sound Brae to the Gilbert Bain to hear what the news was. They were told Jeemsie had lost a lot of blood and was having a transfusion and the others were being treated. They then set off for Scalloway to report.

Needless to say the grenade was never used again. Jeemsie was off work and off Home Guard duty for a long time, but he recovered well. Lowrie was not off long before he was back driving the lorry and Sergeant Hogg did not lose the sight of his eye. If Sergeant Hogg had not moved the semi circle of men behind the peat stacks it could have been a much more serious incident. It probably was the most serious accident in all the Shetland Home Guard Units.

I heard this story from Lowrie quite a few times over the years but had forgot a lot of the detail. One day John George was visiting and I just happened to mention the incident. He could tell me that he was there and so retold the story.

Shooting

There was a twenty-five-yard rifle range at Berry. Some of the young Home Guard boys had fathers who owned .22 rifles so they would take them to the range to practice. Getting bullets, they said, was no problem. One of the boys was Angus Craig who worked at the Scord Quarry. There were some Pioneers working there and they always had plenty of .22 bullets for sale. A box of five hundred bullets cost about fifteen shillings. John told me they fired thousands of shots at the range and of course, with all the practice, they became good shots.

When a shooting competition was held one Sunday morning in 1942, all ten companies in Shetland, from Unst to Sumburgh, took part. The Scalloway company did very well with John George Nicolson getting the gold medal. Scalloway's team, J company, were Jeemsie Thomson, Jimmy Williamson, Jim Smith and John George Nicolson. The range was at the north end of the Clickimin Loch. It was a frosty morning with light showers of snow. Each man had to fire five shots from the 100 yard range with Lee Enfield rifles. All five shots had to be in a four inch circle. After that they moved back to 200 yards and had to shoot for the bull. They were not told their result, but all the succeeding teams were. At the end of the shoot the Scalloway boys knew all the other team's scores but not their own. When they were all gathered together later, the Home Guard Shetland Commander, Sir Arthur Nicolson, announced that he was standing them all tea and cakes in the NAFFI canteen. Speeches were made, tea was drunk and then the gold medal was presented. The Scalloway team, not knowing their scores, were unprepared when it was announced that John had won. He had to be prompted by Jim to go and collect the medal. This was the only time a medal was presented at a shoot. On all subsequent occasions a miniature cup was awarded.

Da Privy

Along the shore in Scalloway, as with a lot of other villages, privies stood in conveniently located spots, built out over the sea. The privy was a necessity, as very few houses had flush toilets and the privies were flushed by the incoming tide. I remember two at West Shore, one at Mid Shore, and one at Blacksness.

Close to the one at Blacksness the Home Guard had a dugout which was used to watch out over the East Voe. One night Angus Craig, John George Nicolson and Jim Smith were in the dugout when they saw an elderly local man enter the privy. The Home Guarders were sixteen-year-old boys and full of mischief. When they thought the elderly local gent was well into his business they pulled lumps of divots and threw on to the privy roof and walls. The boys were still laughing when out charged the infuriated gent, waving a newspaper. They did not hesitate. Armed to the teeth though they were, they left the dugout to a man as if the entire German army was on their tail. Laughing, away along the Bool Green they ran, heavily armed Home Guards chased by an elderly gent waving a newspaper. Ay, you had to be tough to be in the Home Guard.

Da Essy Kert

The year of 1938 saw Scalloway's first essy kert, which was run by John Smith of Berry Farm. It was just an ordinary farm cart painted red and blue (kert colours), with a cover like a roof. There were hatches that could be opened to allow ashes to be tipped in. The cart was pulled by a Berry farm horse called Black Peter, who was supposed to be of Belgian origin.

A possible essy kert.

Farm worker, Magnie Smith was the driver. The operative (or as he was known then, Da Essy Man) was Willie Manson. The collections were two or three days a week. The tip for the refuse was a quarry at the back of Berry which filled rapidly. Everything went fine for a while then Magnie said he had had enough and the operation was terminated.

During the 1930s it was a common thing in Shetland for men to make their own lorries. According to Andy Irvine it was an easy job. You got a Morris Cowley or a Morris Oxford (some were two seaters, with a dickie seat at the back, solidly built), you cut the back part off, fitted a six foot platform, added sides and you had an instant lorry. Andy did this to a Morris he had to

Andy Irvine of Asta, 1955.   © W.S.

make a lorry to cart peats. One day he was in the peat hill filling his lorry when Walter Mowat snr approached from a nearby peat bank. Speaking as the clerk for the Scalloway District Council, Walter said, "Andy, at dis moment we hae nae essy kert in Scalloway an hit being wartime we hae a crisis on wir hands. Looking at dis peerie larry o dine, I tink hit just might be da job for lifting da ess. Does du tink du wid consider taking on da job?"

Andy duly considered and decided to do it. The pay for three collections a week, Monday, Wednesday and Friday (more than we have now), was the magnificent sum of twelve pounds per month; one pound per essy run which occupied the best part of a day. Out of this large sum of money Andy had to pay licence, insurance and petrol. Of course, as Andy says, everything was so much cheaper then. You thought in ten bob notes, certainly not in ten pound notes. The amazing thing was, said Andy, he was able to save some money.

The district council hired the services of Willie Manson, originally from Quarff, for any small job around the village. A cooper to trade, but retired, he was persuaded to go with Andy on the essy kert. He was with Andy for two or three years. Thereafter Andy did the job himself until presumably the Zetland County Council took over from the district council.

At the back of the Blacksness fish sheds a concrete wall had been built out over part of the Sally rocks. The inshore space was where the ashes and rubbish was dumped, so Andy and Willie reclaimed a large piece of ground. (During the mid and later part of the war large pieces of wrecked planes, Catalinas etc. were stored here before being shipped south.) When this area was full they started to fill the area below the Scord quarry, where the former bus company Shalder Coaches had garages, and the new Scord road.

At the war's end the military dumped lots of goodies there which locals, with much rivalry, made sure was not covered over with refuse. Andy tells of a boy, who used to travel with him on his rounds, finding a beautiful compass in perfect working order. Andy did a great job and we boys would watch as he drove along with his essy kert, painted red and blue, just like the crofters kerts.

At one point of the war a German invasion was expected from Norway. If this happened then the words Blood Red would be passed from camp to camp to signify that the Germans had landed. A local wag composed a piece of poetry for the occasion and it goes like this.

> Blood Red has gone, the guard is called, the soldiers
>   all stand to,
> For someone saw the quaintest sight, all painted red
>   and blue.
> A Nazi tank, Von Hindenberg is here himself for
>   cert,
> But half a mo it's Manson, with the Asta Essy Kert

The Funeral

On the 21st July, 1940, at the home of her son in Lerwick, Auntie Baabie of Houss died. She was the wife of the late John William Smith Snr. who was a brother to my father and Uncle Robbie. Going to the funeral in Burra Isle were my brother Tammie, my brother-in-law Clement and Uncle Robbie. It was decided that I, a 12-year-old school-boy, should also go, to represent my sisters. I had never been at a funeral before so it was to be a new experience for me.

On the day of the funeral we went to Blacksness pier where Jemsie Williamson, or as he was better known, Jemsie o Papil, was waiting for us with the white launch, the *Resplendent*. We went aboard. Two men were sitting in the cabin. They were Auntie Baabies sons, Bobby Arthur Smith from Lerwick, and John William Smith Jnr. Tammie, Clement and Uncle Robbie all shook hands with them and I thought I had better do the same. Then we all sat down and Jemsie set off for Papil.

I do not remember anything about going ashore at Papil, but I don't think there was a pier. We all went to a house. I think it was to Jemsie's father and mother, but I'm not sure about that.

There were several people in the house

Jemsie o Papil's "White Launch", 1930s. © C.J.W.

and they were horrified to learn that I, a school boy, was going to the funeral. No, no, they said, he is far too young to attend funerals. That would not do at all, he had better stay here with us. I can remember feeling extremely annoyed at this. After all, had I not travelled all the way from Scalloway to attend the funeral? Needless to say I was over-ruled and after a cup of tea the men set off to the funeral.

A boy about my own age, Andy Smith, whom I knew from previous trips to Papil, was also there so he and I played round about while the men were at the funeral. I had to be careful as I was wearing my Sunday best suit. After the men came back we had a meal before once again boarding the *Resplendent* for the run home to Scalloway. Arriving home I complained bitterly that the Burra folk would not let me go to the funeral.

The Monk's Stone

Willie and Grace Fullerton and their family stayed at West Shore before moving to a new house at Meadowfield. My sister Anna and I were friendly with the family. Whenever they went to Papil to visit Grace's sister Maggie and her family, we usually went too. On one particular visit, John Fullerton and I did not get past the kirn standing in the porch. It was full of "blaand", a most refreshing drink, and we took turns to drink from a ladle. Wondering where we were, John's Aunty Maggie came to look for us. When she saw us at the kirn she said, "Boys you will be swinklin."

It was on one of these occasions, in 1942, that we saw the Monk's Stone. The local gravedigger, Jerry Jamieson, had found it while digging a grave in an old part of the yard. He had cleaned it and set it in a lambs' house and we looked at it and wondered who had carved it, and when. Many were the questions we asked each other, but there were no answers.

The stone was brought to Lerwick, and for many years was in the lobby of the County Buildings. It is now in the Shetland Museum in Lerwick and is called the Monk's Stone.

Soldier, Lowrie Jamieson, Rev Tubby Clayton, Willie Jamieson, Donnie Jamieson, Norwegian, Gibbie Smith and soldier with Monk's Stone, 1942. © *C.J.W.*

It may have been on a day we were there that the Rev Philip (Tubby) Clayton from Toc H visited Papil and had his picture taken. With him were three soldiers, a Norwegian who ferried the party to Burra and some Papil men. It was wartime but the Senior Naval Officer at Lerwick provided the transport. The reason I have these photographs is that Clement Williamson was the photographer. In 1966 the Rev Philip Clayton wrote a

Rev. Tubby Clayton at the church of St. Lawrence, Papil, built in 1815. © *C.J.W.*

letter to Clement. In it he wondered where the stone now was. "I humbly hope," he wrote, "it is retained in Scalloway or Lerwick. I feared it might go down to Edinburgh."

Landing Imminent

The telephones in Scalloway were operated from the telephone exchange in the post office at Blacksness. The post mistress was Gladys Copland who, with her husband Basil, ran the post office and exchange. Basil had a great sense of humour and was quick to turn words around, as he did when a lady called to post a parcel. As she laid the parcel on the counter she said, "I am glad to get that out of my hand." "Where is the parcel going?" asked Basil. "Its Heylor, Northmavine," she replied. Quick as a flash Basil said, "Na, na, put you it to Northmavine, we have no postal service to yon other place."

After the fall of Norway and the build up of German troops there, it was thought that an invasion of Shetland would be next. A massive build up of soldiers took place and camps were established at many locations, including Scalloway. Gladys and Basil got orders one day that the telephone exchange had to be manned 24 hours a day, so that a message (Blood Red), could be quickly passed to the various camps around Scalloway. While it lasted this was very taxing for them.

Basil was sitting one night, half sleeping, with elbow resting on the exchange when a call came through. He answered with a hello. It was High Command. "Pass this message immediately to the Royal Artillery, Berry Camp, the Hospital, Air Sea Rescue Unit and the Home Defence. Enemy landings imminent." "Good grief," said Basil, "is that correct?" "Yes," was the reply, "get the message out immediately." "Thank God for that," said Basil, "this 24 hour working will soon all be over now." That was all that mattered to Basil. A high command officer was no different from any ordinary soldier who visited the post office.

Woodwork Class

The Scalloway Methodist Minister at this time was Pastor William Dexter. Before joining the ministry he had trained and worked as a cabinetmaker. In the early 40s he decided to start a woodwork class and got premises from Nicolson and Co. It was a workshop where William Gray used to make buoys for the herring boats. Pastor Dexter got benches and lots of tools with a grant from somewhere and over a dozen men and boys joined the class. I made a plant stand, old fashioned by today's standards, but just the job at that time. Later I made a stool for piano or organ. When I made the seat for the stool I used plywood from an old tea chest with Ceylon Tea written on it. Wood had to be scrounged from wherever it could be found. I got instructions and a scraper and was told to scrape until the words were removed. A tedious job but I scraped away.

The Dexters were just like everyone else and invited sodgers to their home. This particular evening Mr Dexter had a sodger with him at the class. The sodger was a friendly man who wandered around and

Furniture made at Pastor William Dexter's class, 1943.   © C.J.W.

talked to everyone. When he reached me he asked what I was doing and I said I was getting the ply ready for the seat frame. "Looks like you are ready to glue the ply on," he said. "Go and fetch the glue pot and I will give you a hand." I tried to say that I had to scrape off Ceylon first but he said it was fine. I fetched the glue pot and he brushed on the glue. He then held the ply in place until I put a few pins in.

At that moment Mr Dexter arrived. He looked at the plywood glued to the frame, looked at me and said, "Oh Bill, Bill what have you done? I thought I said you were to scrape off Ceylon before gluing the ply on." The sodger melted away to the far end of the shop and I of course said nothing but just listened to Dexter's wrath. After Mr Dexter went on his way some of the other boys said I should tell him it was the sodger, but I said what did it matter. Ceylon was on the stool during its lifetime.

At the end of the class we had a showing in the Home Guard Nissen hut on Burnett's Station and people came to marvel and exclaim at the fine and splendid things we had made.

The Cook House

The military took over Adie's Store and the north part of Adie's Station. After the war this was occupied by Thomas Smith & Son, Building Contractors, and David Howarth building boats. One day the Royal Engineers arrived on Adie's Station. They set up moulds and ran a large concrete platform. After that they came with two huge cooking ranges. Then they came with hut sections and built a fine cookhouse.

The lower part of Adie's Store was partitioned to make two dining halls. One was for the regular army boys and the other for the Shetland Home Defence. On the upper floor at street level Uncle Robbie had a small part for a workshop. The remainder became a canteen for a time.

By that time chocolate was in very short supply, so if we had a few coppers we used to ask a sodger to go in and buy us a bar. No-one ever refused. Eventually it closed, and was used by The Shetland Bus people. It was great excitement to watch all the goings on. As the military presence built up more cooking facilities were required so two huge cooking pots, field kitchens (something like cutch kettles) were set at the east gable of the cookhouse. In these they made soups and stews etc. It always looked and smelled good to hungry boys.

Teatime for da sodgers was 4.30 and we found out that sometimes slices of cake were served. With rationing now biting hard cake seemed very desirable, so we would hang around the cookhouse trying to look hungry. For growing boys that was not very difficult. The cooks were, as far as I recollect, all Shetland Home Defence men. Soon we would hear, "Pssst, want a bit of cake?" We ate many slices of cake at the cookhouse and drank mugs of tea with Nestles condensed milk.

One afternoon I was there on my own watching what was going on when one of the cooks said, "Here's dee a bit o cake for dee ta tak hame wi dee, wir gitting anidder slab o him da morn." A large piece of cake was very acceptable in our house.

Broad beans seemed to feature a lot on the menu, but the quantities that were in the swill bins showed they were not very popular with da sodgers. One day after lunchtime, when the sodger boys had all left, I went in the mess hall where the cooks were having their lunch. One of them said, "Willie, come an hae some denner wi wis." It was pork, broad beans, white loaf and strong sweet tea. As beans were always a favourite food of mine I ate liberally. The folks at home were curious about the noise and blowing off that went on that night plus the resultant bad smell about the house. Needless to say I never told about the cookhouse dinner as it would have been severely frowned on.

There was a sandbagged machine gun post at Nicolson's Pier, which in the event of an air raid, was manned by the cooks. The gun post was removed when the Shetland Bus operation commenced. When the siren went the cooks had to leave whatever they were doing, get on their steel hats and man the post.

One day I was in the cookhouse when the air raid siren went. It was hand operated and on Main Street. The cooks quickly put into effect their training. Some got boxes of ammunition, others got parts of the machine gun and they all ran across Adie's Station, across the Lord's Well beach and to the gun post, myself included. I cannot recollect whether I was frightened or excited, probably a bit of both. The gun was quickly assembled, ammunition fed in and spares kept to hand, then all eyes turned skywards, mine too. One of the men turned and as there was not much room bumped into me. He looked down. "Good God, Willie is in here wi wis." The corporal said, "Well here he will hae ta bide until da all clear goes." It was exciting and seemed ages before the all clear sounded. Then it was back to the cook house for mugs of hot sweet tea and a bit of cake. Aye, the cooks were a real fine bunch of men.

About that same time we were having a play break at school one day and were all out in the playground when we heard the noise of planes. Looking up we saw five German planes flying very low. The men sitting in the rear gun turrets could be seen quite clearly. A lot of boys ran out of the playground towards the knowes of Upper Scalloway to see the planes better. Soon we heard shouts. It was John Gray the headmaster. He was very angry. "You could all have been killed," he said. The five planes flew over the east hill and in over Lerwick.

Milk Delivery

Milk for Scalloway came from the farms of James Pottinger, Asta and James Irvine, Setter. The Setter milk was delivered by Bertie Hughson and I used to go with him on his delivery rounds, mostly on Saturdays. On school holidays I went every day. On Saturday mornings after all the milk had been delivered, Bertie would drop me off at the school and I would walk home.

One morning when I got out of the van and watched him disappear down the Mill Brae I heard the sound of Bren gun carriers. I looked towards the Scord and saw three carriers rounding the south turn, so I thought it would be a good idea to wait and watch. I climbed the grassy bank below Willie Hutchison's house and as they went past I waved to the sodgers sitting in and on the Bren gun carriers. Then I started to walk towards home. Nearing the school I saw a cow get out of the east park, come running along the road and disappear in the schoolhouse gate. I went to look and it was tearing around John Gray's garden trampling over flowers and vegetables. I tried to chase it out the gate but the cow was either cleverer or more stupid than I was and we

Bertie Hughson with the Setter milk van. © *C.J.W.*

Scalloway School and Schoolhouse, 1930s.   © C.J.W.

just ran around in circles. Suddenly a voice said, "What is going on here?" It was Geordie Ross from Thule on his way to the street. I explained what had happened and the two of us finally got the cow out on the road.

As I walked home through Lovers Lane I heard the sound of a Military Band, so I ran to the hall (hospital) where a band was marching and counter marching and playing fine music. Other children were there, so I joined them to march with the band and to listen. A woman came by and said to me, "Dir folk gyaan looking for dee, du's been missing for twa hours." Time passes quickly when you are enjoying yourself. I went home to receive a telling off. That's life.

George Horne with Bren gun carrier.
Courtesy of Elaine Waddell

Escape to Scotland

One fine frosty night with not a breath of wind, our folks heard a voice calling for help. They put the light out, took down the blackout and opened the window. We all peered out but because it was dark nothing could be seen. Our window overlooked the harbour and that was where the voice was coming from. Soon there was the sound of running footsteps and two men ran by the end of the road. We did not know what was going on but soon heard the splash of oars rowing quickly. Later we heard the story.

The two men were Tommy Watt and John Willum Slater. They launched a boat from the west beach and rowed toward the cries. It was so dark all they could see was the mareel from someone splashing. A soldier had taken Willie Fullerton's small nine foot boat and was going to row to the Scottish mainland. What he did not realise was that Shetland men, when they beach a boat, take out the nile (cork) to let out any water. He had not got very far when the boat foundered and he, a nonswimmer, cried out for help.

Tommy and John Willum soon got hold of him and headed for the slopes at Nicolson's Pier. Quite a crowd had now gathered and willing hands soon hauled the sodger on to dry land. Among the crowd was my cousin, Jamie Alick Watt, to whom I am indebted for the details. The sodger was wet, cold and sick, so Bob Moore ran to his house and came back with some brandy. This was duly administered to the sodger and John Willum was heard to remark, "What a waste of good brandy. He does not deserve it, you should be giving the brandy to Tommy and me." The military soon arrived and took the sodger away. Later in the week his commanding officer sent a letter of thanks to Tommy and John Willum for their prompt action, which undoubtedly saved the sodger's life.

Bob Smith (Dobbel).   © *J.G.N.*

A training exercise at the East Voe, to learn how to ferry an injured man across a river proved fatal for one poor sodger. With full kit on he was tied to a poorly constructed raft and towed across the Voe. Somehow he slipped off the raft and with the weight of his full kit disappeared below the water. I suppose they tried to look for him, but nothing was found.

Word soon spread around the village and early next morning Bob Smith (better known as Dobbel) and Willie Hutchison took a boat and rowed over the area. Using a water glass they saw the sodger lying on the bottom. They lowered a hook and brought the body ashore, then informed the military. There was an inquest and Bob and Willie were called. When Willie was being questioned he was asked what he thought was the cause of the accident. It was quite obvious Willie said. The officers in charge were incompetent, poorly trained and did not fully understand what they were doing

The Hospital

Scalloway Public Hall was taken over by the military and became a hospital run by the Royal Army Medical Corps. We always understood it was the main military hospital for Shetland. Da Peerie Hall was used as an operating theatre and everything was painted gloss white. The woodwork in Da Peerie Hall was pitch pine. I remember us after the war scraping the white paint off, not the best of jobs.

An extension was built on the west side and in a room there was an X-ray unit. The walls and ceiling of the room were lined with sheet lead. Lots of huts were built near the hall for wards, cookhouse etc. and one was surrounded with barbed wire and referred to, we understood, as the pox ward. One of the doctors on that ward was called Captain Treacher. The head of the hospital at the start of the war, and for some time, was Major Fox. Dr Treacher, his wife and a little dog called Whisky stayed in Roselyn beside Tammie and Lizzie Smith. Later Dr Chisolm,

Scalloway Public Hall.   © C.J.W.

his wife and son Derek stayed there too. Tammie was my brother and had the firm of Thomas Smith and Son.

Nissen huts were built in what is now Gibblestone Road. The hut construction farthest north had lots of chairs and seats where the staff could relax. A film van visited about once a fortnight and when any of us boys asked to get in we were never refused. We would rush there after school and many a film we saw.

A Nissen hut also stood where the Royal British Legion car park is now sited. One day when we were going back to school after dinner we saw the hut door open. Always curious we looked in and there we saw two trestle tables. Behind the tables stood a sodger, but on the tables what a sight met our eyes. Bars of chocolate, bags of pandrops, biscuits, fags, matches and lots more. The sodger said, "Hi boys come away in." We asked if this was a shop. "Oh yes, it's a shop all right but just for the hospital staff and patients." Someone asked if we could buy anything if we had money. "Of course, I'll sell you anything you want, no bother, as long as no one is watching."

The Nissen hut shop was open for a few months, then, one day it was closed. It was probably moved inside the complex somewhere, out of sight of small boys, which was a great pity. While it was open how-

Scalloway Military Hospital staff, 1942. © C.J.W.

Last of the hospital wards, 1950s. © C.J.W.

ever we bought chocolate, pandrops and of course, Woodbines, whenever we had money. The sodger was always pleased to see us and would yarn away. An old threepence bought a bar of chocolate and one and three bought fags. Happy days.

At the north end of this hut was the fumigation unit. A sodger would hang blankets etc. in there then light two huge blowlamps. The heat was directed into the unit and presumably the heat killed off any bugs hanging around. One day we watched the sodger and he was having problems with one of the blowlamps. It kept flaring up with lots of flame. It was very exciting. When the problem was sorted out the sodger, poor fellow, was minus his eyebrows and eyelashes.

Lots of the regiments stationed in Scalloway gave Christmas parties for the school children and they were much appreciated by all. The Royal Army Medical Corps. Christmas parties were special. I suppose that is why I remember them best of all. There was always an abundance of food to eat and their parties were not to be missed. For the party, the beds were cleared from the large ward in the main hall and decorations put up. We never realised or thought what a bother they went to, just to give us children a party. They were great guys and enjoyed the parties as well. We had games and singing with some sodgers doing a turn of some kind. There were always presents and a visit from Santa Claus, who I remember one time was Major Fox, the senior medical officer.

At one party we were told our photo was going to be taken. Clement Williamson arrived just before the party ended, carrying a tripod and all sorts of cameras and gear. We were all gathered together at the stage end of the hall. Clement set up the tripod, fixed his camera and with a lot of effort we were all got in place ready for the photo. There was no fancy flash equipment at that time. When Clement got the camera in focus he took the flashgun, which was about twelve inches long and placed some magnesium powder on the tray. There was a trigger under which he placed a cap as used in toy cap guns. Then someone put out most of the lights, Clement opened the camera shutter, held the flashgun aloft and shouted, "Everyone look this way. Smile," and let go the trigger. There was a bang from the cap, a whoosh from the powder and as you can see, a good photo. It was almost sixty years ago. How time flies.

Many people invited soldiers, sailors, airmen and Norwegians into their homes during an evening and our family was no exception. Some of the soldiers who visited were from the Royal Army Medical Corps at the hospital. Jack Speirs from Edinburgh, George Reid from Rutherglen, Staff Sergeant Rattery (everybody called him Staff, I'm not sure where he came from) and George Redpath from Edinburgh. George Redpath helped us at the peat hill raising the peats. He once said he would bring some sandwiches to have with our tea (tea in the peat hill always tasted much better) and we thought that would be fine. His sandwiches,

Christmas party at the hospital, 1942.   © C.J.W.

however, caused some amusement, but I did enjoy them. They were about one and a half inches thick, liberally spread with butter and, joy of joys, packed with thick slices of tomato. If I had been allowed to I would have eaten them all.

The RAMC men like all soldiers, always carried gas masks and steel helmets wherever they went. One night, as well as his gas mask Jack had a small kit bag with him which he set beside his chair. When it came time for tea, the table was set with cups, plates and knives, white loaf, rhubarb jam and biscuits, or whatever we had in the house (after all there was a war going on). Just before tea was poured Jack asked if we had a tin opener and a large plate. This was produced and he took a tin out of his kit bag. It was as round as a large soup tin but longer. He opened the tin and emptied the contents onto the large plate; jellied chicken fillets. We had a super supper that night. Before they left, Jack took another tin from the kit bag and said we were to have it for our lunch tomorrow, but remember, not a word. They got more supplies than could be used, he said, and it was just dumped. Our meagre rations were supplemented on various occasions and we never said a word.

One year just after Christmas time, when some local men were working at the hospital, one of the cooks came to them with a large basket and gave everyone a roast chicken. Needless to say the men were delighted and families had a Christmas dinner all over again.

John George Nicolson told me of an incident at the hospital where, as a young lad, he worked with Uncle Robbie painting windows. There were no slick extension ladders in those days. The ladders came in various lengths and were heavy. While painting the upstair windows and moving the ladder from one window to the next, they did not lower it down but carried it, balanced perpendicularly between them. All went well for a while, then, at the next move the ladder hit one of the electric wires. They stopped and looked up. John said a ripple was going along the wire from pole to wall and back again.

As they looked up an officer came around the corner, smartly dressed, complete with brown gloves and a little cane. When he saw John and Uncle Robbie gazing upwards, he did likewise. Then he spoke. "Who did that? If I knew who did that, I'd kick his arse." John said he suddenly found himself holding the ladder alone and Uncle Robbie's nose was about two inches from the officer's nose. Uncle

Robbie said, "We did it, not intentionally, but my boy, if du wants tae keek arses just du mind at two can play at dat game." The officer beat a hasty retreat rather than have his arse kicked by a wrathful Uncle Robbie.

On another occasion John, Willum Hughson from Weisdale and Uncle Robbie were sent to repaint one of the many wards. The ceiling and top half of the walls were cream distemper and the bottom was green paint. A one inch black line divided the two. The distemper came as a thick paste and had to have water added and stirred. This could take a little time. They had galvanised pails for this job and when they were finished at night the pails were just left for the next day, as distemper did not have to be lidded like oil paint.

When the time came to start painting the one inch line on the finished walls the job was given to John. On the morning of this story John got his brush and black paint and made a start. Uncle Robbie got his distemper stirred, added a little more water and also made a start. Not so Willum, he stirred and he better stirred.

After a while John heard Willum say, "Robbie, I can't understand it, dis is cream distemper bit dir broon grunds in da boddam o my bucket."

Workmen at the hospital. Willum Hughson, Robbie Mouatt, ?, John George Nicolson, Uncle Robbie, George Nicolson, ?, 1940. *Courtesy of John G. Nicolson*

John and Uncle Robbie went to look. After an inspection of Willum's stirring stick, broon grunds and bucket they came to the conclusion that sometime overnight someone had dropped a large turd in the bucket.

Uncle Robbie was furious and taking the bucket and stirring stick headed for the door. John and Willum moved to a window. Uncle Robbie went striding across the road towards the main hospital. On the way he met Staff Sergeant Langdon and John said they could see the stick with the broon grunds on it waving under his nose. Backing off smartly the Staff Sergeant pointed to the main door. Uncle Robbie went to Major Fox's office and delivered an opinion as to the type of person who would do such a thing. Telling me this story many years later, John said, "Du kens Willie, dy Uncle Robbie wis never pitten tae use bad wirds, bit du sood a heard him dat day."

The Barber Shop

Tammy Thomson had a hairdressing shop in front of the Methodist Chapel. The far end of the shop was where he repaired boots and shoes. Like many Shetland men of his time he was good at whatever he did and he was good at both trades.

Tammie's byword was, "Come an I'll mak dee bonnie." In the summer he would give the young boys what he called his simmer clip. This meant the clippers starting at the back of the neck and stopping just short of the forehead. I never had a simmer clip. My hair, just like some young boys at times, had got rather long and I was always too busy, or so I said, to go and get it cut.

Tammy Thomson's hairdressing shop.
© *C.J.W.*

One Saturday morning I was given money and ordered, not asked, to go and see Tammy. When I got there a lot of men and sodgers were sitting on the long bench. I squeezed myself on to the bench alongside a sodger. Tammy turned to see the new customer, gave me a second look, and said to me, "Peerie boy, can du read?" I replied that I could indeed read. "Well dan," Tammy said, "go and read yon notice in my window." The notice I read was as follows, "No bairns' hair cuts on Saturdays." So I went home, not very pleased I should add.

One day through the week I was again told to go and see Tammy. This I flatly refused to do and nothing could persuade me. "If he can't cut my hair on Saturday," I said, "then every other day is the same." The stalemate ensued for several weeks. My hair, by now, was down over my neck and over my eyes but still I would not go.

One day a sodger came into Clement's Photographic Studio (Clement was my brother-in-law). In the course of conversation the sodger said he was a hairdresser to trade and was their company barber. I remember sodgers having their hair cut, sitting on a stool in Meadowfield Crescent. The sodgers name was Sammy Bates. On hearing he was a hairdresser Clement said to Sammy, "Would you do me a favour and cut my young brother-in-law's hair? He will not go to the barber."

So it was arranged that I should be at Clement and Mary's the next night for my tea, and Sammy would arrive with his clippers etc. about half past six. I, of course, knew nothing about this. Sammy arrived and after some conversation said he had his haircutting tools with him and asked if Clement would like his haircut. Clement agreed and sat down on a chair. Sammy talked away while he was cutting and as he was finishing turned to me and said, "What about you mate? Looks like you could do with a trim. Come and sit in the chair." They all breathed a sigh of relief when I meekly went and sat down and Sammy started to snip away at my long locks. It was quite a while before I went back to Tammy again.

A friend told a story in our house of how he went to Tammy one day for a trim and asked, "Is du been busy da day Tammy?" "Oh yes," says Tammy, "dat am I, min Doctor Treacher wis in dis morning." Our friend thought he did not know who Doctor Treacher was so asked, "What doctor is dat Tammy?" "Oh, du kens him," said Tammy," he's da doctor dat da sodger boys shows dir sore tooties tae."

RAF Castle Camp, 1950s.   © *C.J.W.*

The Castle Camp

The Royal Air Force decided to base two Air Sea Rescue boats at Blacksness. I remember one was much faster than the other. A camp for the crews was needed and it was built on an area of ground north of the castle, where The Wool Company now stands. It was called The Castle Camp. Then they needed a slipway for the boats, so that was built in The Muckle Yard.

My sister Mary and Clement stayed in Blacksness House. Lots of days I would go there after school. My playmates at Blacksness were Billy and Douglas Duncan. For a while we kept an eye on how work was proceeding. I'm sure the workmen would have managed quite well without us but we were not to know that.

There were no great JCB's or mechanical aids, just plain manpower. They dug with picks and shovels, set moulds and mixed concrete. It was hard work. We liked to listen to the banter that went on with the men and we learned some new words I remember. We also learned

Blacksness RAF Air Sea Rescue group, RAF Castle Camp.   © *C.J.W.*

how and where to use them. After the war Capt. Hay used the slip for a short time for fishing boats but then things started to go wrong so it was abandoned.

The ASR boats had two gun turrets. Sometimes the RAF boys on guard would let us on board to climb up into the turrets and blast away at make believe German planes. You sat on a seat, like that of a motorbike, and could whirl the turret round and round with your feet, it was great fun. So the RAF gave us some excitement as well.

They took over Hay & Co. shop premises at Blacksness and had a recreation room upstairs. Sometimes there were film shows and sometimes ENSA shows. We

RAF slipway, Blacksness.   © *C.J.W.*

Castle and last Nissen hut at Castle Camp.
© *C.J.W.*

boys were always made welcome and were seated at the front, sometimes on the floor. We saw musicians, singers and comics but none of them comes to mind.

One ENSA show had a magician. His assistant was a lovely, lively and bouncy young lady. She had long bare legs, tight pants, a nicely rounded bum and very prominent boobs. Even we young boys could see that she came in and out in all the right places, plus she had a captivating smile. She got lots of whistles from the RAF boys but we wouldn't have dared, I think! I don't recall any of the magician's tricks, but I do, after all these years remember the lovely, lively, bouncy young lady and all her bits and pieces moving with such precision.

At the war's end one of the RAF boys, Harry Cole from Yorkshire married a cousin of mine, Elizabeth Watt. They stayed on in Scalloway for a number of years after the war, then moved to Yorkshire. It was Harry who told me about the moving of Johnson's Angel. He also told about one of their trips in the ASR boats.

It was a really bad day and a plane had ditched south of Sumburgh Head. They left Blacksness and headed south into heavy seas. The coxswain that day, said Harry, was a man from Cunningsburgh, George Cogle. When they were in the Roost the boat was being tossed around like a cork. The crew were holding on for dear life and were very relieved to hear a radio message which said: "Return to base, survivors picked up." Harry reckoned that without the sea knowledge of George Cogle they might not have made it back to Scalloway that day.

Jan Harris was also coxswain on the boats at Blacksness. Jan married a local girl, Millie Williamson. They stayed in Scalloway for a number of years then went to Canada. One of the officers, Pilot Officer Bill Garrett, married a girl from Burra Isle, Ruby Ann Inkster.

One evening in the winter of 1944 (I think), between eight and nine o'clock, Mary and Clement arrived at our house. They were carrying some bags and said they had come to stay the night. For some days previously water had been heard dripping in the castle. No one thought much about it until the story got out that, among the military hardware stored within the castle walls, were some kind of Mills bombs. They supposedly had to be kept under water in tanks and now the tanks were leaking. Someone from the Blacksness area contacted the military and the story went, that on examination in the hours of darkness, it was thought there was the risk of an explosion. Anyone who could and wanted to was advised to move out of the area. As far as I remember it was all a false alarm but a bit of excitement. If things had gone differently the castle might now just be a heap of rubble.

Soldiers at Lowrie Mowat's Smiddy, 1940.   © C.J.W.

Robert Irvine uncovers Johnson's carving.
© C.J.W.

The Angel of Peace

Many years ago William Johnson, a Quarff man, built the Noost in Scalloway. Johnson was a mason to trade and also made tombstones, some of which can be seen in Tingwall churchyard. He was well read and could talk on many subjects and was an inventor. He held certain ideas about the tides and published a book "The Law of Universal Balance". A copy can be seen in the Shetland Library.

In 1910 he did a carving on the wall of his house concerning tides and would stand and explain his theories to anyone who would listen. At the first war's end he added to his carving the words, "German Theories Controverted, Germans are not the Favoured of Heaven".

After Johnson's death, whoever was in the house got fed up with people standing reading, discussing and arguing about the inscription so they plastered it over. In the late forties or early fifties Robert Irvine bought the house. Either Clement, or his brother Wilfie, told him about the carving. He would like to see it, he thought, so decided to take the plaster away and spent many long hours doing so. It has deteriorated somewhat now but can still be seen there today and people still stop to read and wonder.

At the end of the first world war Johnson, using sand and cement, made a lifesize model of an angel which he called The Angel of Peace. Johnson purposed it should be erected in Scalloway, carrying the names of the local men and women who lost their lives in the war. To this end a photo was taken and a background and plinth were drawn in. The accompanying picture shows how it would have looked.

Unfortunately this never happened and after William Johnson's death the angel was left in an old workshop. As boys we used to look in through cracks in the door and see the angel lying on a bench. We always felt very much in awe. After all it was an angel.

The RAF boys knew it was there and one night some of them, led by a fed-up corporal, took the angel out of the workshop and carried it, quite a weight it was too, up into the castle, where they placed it in one of the windows overlooking the street. It took them two hours to do this and they thought it a great joke.

However, some of the local people thought it was sacrilegious. After all, it was an angel. Some folk got quite a scare at night when they saw the white angel looking out the castle window. I can remember seeing it there but in the daytime. It was in the castle for forty-eight hours.

The CO, when he heard about it and saw it, was furious. He upbraided the corporal and ordered its immediate removal. A very much chastened corporal rounded up his men and got to work. The angel probably got back to its shed a lot quicker than it left.

It was there at the war's end and at some time after was broken up. It was a sad end to a really artistic piece of work and a really good idea.

William Johnson's carving.   © C.J.W.

William Johnson's Angel of Peace.

© C.J.W.

William Johnson was buried in the churchyard at Quarff. He had a stone in the shape of a heart and carved on it, "Between my mothers grave and mine". This stone was to be placed between his grave and that of his mother. I wonder if it was ever done?

The following poem was written by William Johnson and displayed on his house in Scalloway several times.

Christian base grabber, oh beware,
You'll get your share of blank
despair
When God, who for the sparrows
care
And ask Him to avenge.

There is no pardon for the men
Who crucify the Lord again
And fearful looking for of bane
And wrath that never change.

Oh blinded Kaiser when you were
Baptised to Christ, you promised
there
That you would take His cross,
and bear
The world's most galling crown.

Repent, return, oh be in time
All ye, who share the Kaisers
crime.
It brings on you like damning
rhyme
"Let no man take thy crown."

On Christmas Day, 1918 an effigy of the Kaiser was made and burned with the galley at Garriock's pier. It is believed that the inscription above was destroyed in the flames on Christmas night

Tingwall

An army camp was constructed at the Tingwall crossroads and during the first of the war, when German planes were seen over Shetland quite often, the camp was machine gunned on at least two occasions. The first time, on 14th June, 1941 Sergeant John Knight of the 7th Battalion The Seaforth Highlanders was hit by bullets and died in the military hospital at Scalloway. A native of Granton-on-Spey, he was buried in the Tingwall churchyard on 16th June. Other soldiers were injured and damage was done to buildings and fittings. I started

Address to the Bloody Kaiser, 1918. © *C.J.W.*

to go to funerals in 1946 and in the churchyard, Sergeant John Knight's grave was a lonely one. No longer lonely, he now lies with the good folk of Tingwall and Scalloway all around him.

Workmen from Scalloway went to the camp after the raid to do repairs. John Nicolson and Peerie Jeck Hutchison were there with others. John's father Geordie was in charge. Arriving at the camp an officer told them it was expected the planes would come back. If they heard the air raid siren, they were to run as fast and as far from the camp as they could. Later on through the day the siren went and they dropped tools and ran. John and Jeck ran together along the road towards Saundersfield and crawled under the bridge that spans the burn. There they waited uncomfortably for the all clear to sound. Some considerable while later they heard footsteps on the road. It was Geordie looking for them. The all clear had long been sounded, but under the bridge they never heard it.

It was decided by high command that the Scalloway Home Guard would attack and try to take the Tingwall camp. It was well planned and everyone knew what they had to do, so a night was set on and away they went. Lowrie drove the lorry to the Njuggles Water burn and, disembarking, the platoon set off up and over the hill. They came down the Daal at Veensgarth, all in darkness and made tracks for the camp. Barbed wire surrounded the camp and there were guards, of course, so they sent out scouts. Some sort of wire cutters were attached to their rifles and the scouts used them to good effect, cutting several holes in different places around the sleeping camp. Crawling on their bellies the men entered the camp.

John George Nicolson and Angus Craig were instructed to enter the hut housing the camp's generator and stop the engine. The soldier in charge of the generator took some persuading from Angus to actually stop the engine, but eventually the camp was plunged into darkness. Andy of Asta grabbed one of the guards in a bear hug and frightened the man out of his wits. Andy was a very strong man, and I suppose squeezed the guard more than he meant to. The others threw thunder flashes into the Nissen huts among the sleeping soldiers and, shouting loudly, charged through the huts making a lot of noise. In much less time than it takes to tell, the camp was in the hands of the Scalloway Home Guard. Much to the discomfiture of the camp's officers, the Home Guard Unit was complimented by high command.

The Tingwall Manse was requisitioned for a convalescent hospital for servicemen. Three huts were built for wards and used right up to the end of the war. Shortly after I started work, John George and I did some repairs to doors in one of the wards.

The Studio

Clement J. Williamson, the local photographer, had his studio at New Street, Scalloway. When the war started it did not look good for anyone trying to make a living taking photos. However, Clement got a licence from the authorities to take photos in The Studio and also outside for the military. Soldiers, sailors, Royal Air Force men and Norwegians visited The Studio and had their photographs taken. Some of these photos are in my possession today. Clement could speak Swedish and some Norwegian, so he always had visitors. He made many friends and often invited them to Blacksness House to while away an evening.

One day a local man who was working at the Scatsta aerodrome came into The Studio and asked Clement if he would copy a photo for him. Clement agreed, and asked to see the photo. The photo was of RAF Flying Boats lying at anchor in Sullom Voe. Clement just about had kittens, "Get that out of my studio at once. Do you want me to lose my licence? Where did you get that?" The man said he had borrowed it from the office he was working in and would have to get it back next day before it was missed.

On another occasion four soldiers came and wanted their picture taken together. When they left, one of Clement's best cameras left with them. He never saw it again.

Clement J. Williamson, 1930s. © *C.J.W.*

Clement, Mary and Jimmy James, 1944.

Concerts

When the nation held Wings For Victory week and everyone was urged to part with as much cash as they were able for the war effort, the ASR boats did trips to the isles and back for two shillings or a half crown. This was a great thrill. We were able to see the Royal Artillery gun sites at Port Arthur. During Wings For Victory week there was a concert in the West Shore Netloft, later Norway House. I well remember the singing and trumpet playing of a soldier. For one so young, I was very impressed and he really opened my ears to music. The wireless was in great demand after this and I listened to as much music as I could.

There were many professional musicians drafted into the services. A lot were in Scalloway and could be seen and heard at concerts. I remember a fine four stringed banjo player. He was a good player but had a funny quirk about his mouth while he played. What a lovely sound the banjo had. That was what I wanted, but we had no money for banjos. I suppose we were lucky to eat.

I got a biscuit tin, nailed a piece of wood to it, got four old fiddle strings from Uncle Robbie and made my own banjo. Everyone thought it a good laugh to hear me play my banjo and sing. The song was "Way down upon the Swanee river", with no fancy chords, just whatever I could find among the fiddle strings. Those were happy days.

Some of the regiments had pipe bands and some had military bands. They would march and play in the area before the hall and on the Burn Beach. Soldiers would parade and sergeants would shout. They were exciting times.

There were many film shows and concerts in the West Shore Netloft and later in the old United Free Church, at the time in use as a Church of Scotland canteen. I remember a play with John Gray our Headmaster, Gracie Henry the infant teacher, Amie Hunter and Lolly Young. Other local people took part as well as servicemen. Concerts were talked about for days after. I remember two soldiers doing a comic turn and was puzzled by the adults laughing at sayings we did not understand or find funny. Well, that was until some of the older boys explained!

Towards the end of the war there was a typhoid scare in the village and the medical authorities advised people not to gather together or attend any sort of social event. One night two friends and I were walking along Main Street when we met the Congregational minister Mr Hamilton. He asked if we were going to the film show at the RAF at Blacksness. We replied that people were not supposed to gather together owing to the typhoid scare so there would not be any film show tonight. He said, "Well boys, I wonder. Yes I wonder. Come, we will all go and see what we can see."

So to Blacksness the four of us went. Upstairs in Hay's shop was the RAF recreation room where they showed films. We were just in time. The film had started. It was called *Blythe Spirits*. A corporal directed us to seats and the minister had a good look round. He noted several local dignitaries and military officers in the audience. He leaned over to us and said, "Well boys, so much for the typhoid scare. Enjoy the film."

It was a good film and we did enjoy it. At the end a local dignitary stood up and gave a vote of thanks to the RAF boys for putting on the show and everybody clapped. The minister stood up and made for the door, the three of us following. At the door, in a loud voice he said, "Its nice to know that when a gathering is forbidden, people observe and obey that." This was of course a strong hint to the members of his congregation and the local bigwigs who were present.

On one occasion when money was being raised for Wings For Victory week, there were to be two nights of concerts in the Netloft. Forms were set at the front for bairns, and there were lots of bairns seated on them. At the end of one act the bairns cheered and with all the acts following, cheered louder. Every bairn tried to see who could cheer loudest. I remember it well. No one was doing any harm. The bairns (I was a bairn too) were enjoying themselves, after all it was supposed to be a jolly occasion, but it was quite a noisy racket. Some local busybody however, thought it was not quite the thing. Next day at school, John Gray the Headmaster announced that no bairns were to be allowed at the second concert. It was a bit tough on the war effort as lots of parents did not bother going if they could not take their bairns.

The Baby Seal

One Sunday morning a lone baby seal swam along the shore making mewing sounds. One of the RAF boys heard him and somehow got a hold of him. He carried the young seal up the brae to the Castle Camp and the whole unit turned out to see it. Someone said, "Lets make it our

Sammy the Seal.   © *C.J.W.*

mascot," and so it was agreed. Then came the problem as to how to feed it. It would not take milk from a feeding bottle. It was suggested they get a ewe, but that was no use either. The baby seal now had a name, Sammy. Word spread quickly around the village. A baby seal was in the Castle Camp and soon a crowd of boys and others were heading to have a look.

The Commanding Officer said, "We will have to get it fed, it won't take milk you say?" The answer was, "No sir, it won't take milk." "What about the ewe?" asked the officer. Again the answer was in the negative. "What about soup then, have you tried that?" "Yes sir, we tried the soup, but no use." "Strange," said the officer, "it was good soup." "Excuse me sir," said a corporal, "but if the seal is going to be our mascot you will have to burn the soup first before it will appreciate it." There was much laughter from all.

Someone had been at the pier and come with sillocks. The same corporal noticed that the seal made sucking noises on a sillock. He then devised a method to feed the baby seal, which proved highly successful. He gutted and split a sillock and rolled it up like a small tube. As the seal sucked on the fish, milk was gently poured through the tube and the seal gulped it down. The RAF boys dug and made a small pool for the seal to wallow in and he slept in a peerie felly house. With plenty of milk and fresh fish the seal got bigger and fatter. We used to go and splash at the pool and play with Sammy. We were told that when all the bairns had gone home he would cry and make blubbing noises, just like a bairn, until a member of the unit would run and pick him up and cuddle him. As he grew older he would waddle down Blacksness Brae to the sea and swim around where the fishing boats were.

Walter Smith from Hamnavoe told me that one time, when home on leave, he was asked to go off with the *Homeland* to the herring. One morning they had landed at Blacksness Pier and as he was going to the shops, in Walter's words, "Man, I could hardly believe my eyes, a young selkie coming waddling down Blacksness Brae. I thought it very strange. When I came back to the boat, there was the seal on the pier and the men were filleting herring with their fingers and throwing to the seal." Sammy would regularly go to the boats, Walter said, as he certainly liked herring.

Poor Sammy did not live to reach maturity. When only about half grown, he got a lung infection. An RAF doctor examined him. It was pneumonia and Sammy died after a couple of days. He had become part of the unit and part of the village as well and was mourned by all. He gave a lot of pleasure to the RAF boys and to the bairns who visited the camp regularly to play and pet the baby seal.

Berry Camp

Berry Camp, 1940s. © C.J.W.

Berry Camp was not in our area, so I do not have much to say about it. I was in the camp on one occasion. My brother Tammie was going to do a small job so took me along to carry bits of wood and pass tools, nails etc. to him. At the gate we were challenged by the guard. Tammie had a pass but I was just waved through. The job took about two hours.

The first soldiers to occupy the camp were the Staffords. Georgie Duthie told me they arrived on the 6th December (I can't remember what year) and every pipe was frozen solid. She said the family felt so sorry for the young men. Berry Camp, like other camps, had a recreation hut and would get a film show from ENSA about once a fortnight. On one occasion the Fullerton family got an invite to come and see a film. The young ones went, but halfway through something broke down and they never found out how the film ended.

One day the sergeant major took men drilling in Meadowfield Crescent. As was his wont, he shouted and roared at the men. He called them all kinds of names for not doing exactly as he wanted. Suddenly an elderly lady appeared, and in a voice that could be heard all over the Crescent, she upbraided the sergeant major. She told him he could not speak to the poor boys like that and was to stop it immediately. The

Soldiers in Meadowfield Crescent. © C.J.W.

Soldiers in Meadowfield Crescent, 1940.   © C.J.W.

poor boys had to hide their amusement, as to be seen smiling would have brought more wrath upon them.

Two girls (one was a Bressay lass) from the Berry Camp NAFFI canteen used to visit Mrs Smith at Berry farm. One day, one of the girls said that a soldier kept bringing eggs to get cooked, large eggs with spots, the like of which she had never seen before. They had never asked and did not know where the eggs came from. Mrs Smith laughed and said, "That's turkey eggs. My daughter Eva has a pet turkey and we have been wondering about the absence of eggs." It transpired that the turkey had a nest between an old house and the byre. The soldier had stumbled on this, a good source of nourishment.

Peerie Charlie

Up at the top of Houll lived an old man called Peerie Charlie. I think his surname was Williamson, but I'm not sure. He was never what you could call clean. He was always dirty looking, at least that's how I remember him. He had a coal fire as did most people. Nicolson and Co. sold coal and Charlie would buy a quarter bag at the time as it was a long way up the brae to Houll (he carried the bag on his back). Late one winter afternoon at the first of the war, Charlie went to Nicolson's for his rations. When he left the shop it was dark and with the black outs there were no lights anywhere. About five o'clock, Lolly Dalgleish the shop owner, would always take his torch and do a tour of the sheds to check they were all locked up. This night he had checked the coal store and was passing the slopes when he thought he heard a sound.

He stopped, listened, then called out, "Anyone there?" Again he heard the sound, it was coming from seaward. Thoughts of German invaders went through his mind, but bravely he beamed the torch seaward. There, standing in about three feet of water, was Charlie. Lolly directed him to the slope and helped him ashore. "Just lost me rod du kens," was all he said. Some men who were in the shop went home with Charlie and helped him into dry clothes and got him warmed up.

Nicolson and Company

I started work as a part-time message boy with Nicolson & Co., West Shore, Scalloway, when I was twelve years old and we were into the second year of the war. Nicolson & Co. were general merchants and the owner was Lolly Dalgleish. Also working in the shop were Lolly's wife Carrie, Meenie Nicolson from Houl, my sister Chrissie, Pearl Mouatt, Ada Laurenson, Billy Thomson and Willie Isbister who went with the shop van to country areas and was later in the RAF.

To begin with I accompanied Billy Thomson on the message rounds. On one occasion we were on our way to a house and Billy was smoking a fag. He put his hand holding the fag into his jacket pocket before we came to the house door. The woman took the basket of messages and went in. Billy then took a few puffs at his fag and blew the smoke in the open door. When the woman came back she sniffed the air and said, "Is there someone smoking?" "Not me," I said, and held out my hands. Billy said, "Not me," and held out both his hands. The woman looked puzzled. "Very strange, I could have sworn I smelled fag reek." She spoke to us for a moment or two before we left. Once around the corner I asked, "What happened tae da fag?" "In here," said Billy, who was looking in his pocket at the hole burned through his jacket lining.

All the groceries came in bulk – tea, sugar, oatmeal, flour, butter and cheese. Sometimes I would be set on to weigh and bag or wrap the various items. As everything was rationed the weight had to be precise. However this did not prevent the odd small bit of cheese from finding its way into my mouth.

Treacle

Crofter folk would sometimes come with a pail and ask for cows treacle. The treacle was kept in a large barrel in the lower store and was sold by the half gallon. I enjoyed the trips to the store, measuring and getting the treacle. I suppose it was because I always dipped a finger in and took a lick. I once returned from the store with treacle and was asked, "Is the treacle good today?" which made everyone laugh. I only understood the laughter when I looked in the mirror and saw treacle on my chin.

Breaking Wind

Once a week I delivered messages to an old lady who stayed in the Back Road. She always wore the same clothes; a dark coloured skirt almost to her ankles, a wrap around peenie and a moorit hap over her head and shoulders. She must have been housebound, as I cannot recall ever having seen her outside her home. Anyway, I was told to just open her door, walk in and put the messages from the basket onto the table. Having done this, I said, "Here's your messages from the shop." The old lady said, "Thank you," rose from her seat at the fireside and moved to the table. The strain of rising caused her to break wind and as she walked to the table, every step she took was followed by a loud fart. Few twelve-year-old boys would have been able to keep their composure under such circumstances. I was not one of them. I howled with laughter and then my face went pink. Thankfully the old lady did not seem to mind and just spoke away as normal. Now, much later in life, I realise she could not help it any more than I, perhaps, can myself.

Puddens

One day Lolly said, "Willie, go to the store and find a box from Mellis and see if there are any puddings in it." I went to the store, found the box and looked in but could see no puddings. Back at the shop, I told Lolly, "There are no puddings in the box." He shook his head, "Oh dear, dear. They were supposed to send them and they are on the invoice. Well, what did you find in the box?" I said, "There was so and so and such and such and two dozen mealy puddens." "I see," he said, without a vestige of a smile. "Will you go and take the puddens here to me?" I had always understood that pudding was what we had after dinner, and puddens was what we sometimes had at teatime. No doubt Lolly had a smile later – a true gentleman he was.

Yellow Chrome

We sold paint in the shop. Most of it was by the firm of Peacock and Buchan, Southampton. The tins of paint were delivered in big barrels and packed with sawdust. When the barrel arrived every tin had to be brushed and dusted before being set on the shelves. On one occasion while doing this, a tin of yellow chrome slipped through my fingers and fell onto the concrete floor. Of course the lid came off. I went down very fast after the tin and saved about half. I was pouring sawdust over the mess when Lolly came through the door. Looking at him fearfully I said, "I'm drappit a tin." He looked at the mess. "Oh well, clean it as best you can," was all he said.

Charles Nicolson with cups, 1930s. © *C.J.W.*

The shop must have sold quite a lot of paint because Charles Nicolson, one of the family members of Nicolson & Co. was, I believe, influential regarding the presenting by Peacock & Buchan of a beautiful sailing boat trophy to the Scalloway Yacht club. It was to be competed for at the local regatta. The photo shows Charlie Nicolson with the trophies he won sailing his boat *Seagull*. She was a 14ft haddock boat built by Tammas Walter Scott for Tammy Thomson of Nort Ness, Trondra.

Peerie Pheelie

One day I saw a little black ball run across the floor of the shop, stopping when it hit the counter. There were a lot of people in the shop but I went outside the counter and picked the object up out of curiosity. I held it up to see what it was, when suddenly Carrie leaned across the counter and smacked me across the hand, knocking the ball from my grasp. "Go and wash your hand," she said. She followed me to the basin in the backshop, laughing. "Do you know what that was you picked up?" "No," I said, washing my hands. "Did you see Peerie Pheelie in the shop? Well, she chews tobacco and what you picked up was her discarded plug which she had just spit out on the floor." I washed my hands furiously.

Four and a Half Dozen

On Mondays after school I delivered messages to the Hornes of Blydoit. I always liked going to Blydoit – it was a fine long walk and Mrs Horne would give me a large glass of milk and a jam sandwich. As they usually got a big basket of messages, I would take the shop barrow. It had two wheels and was a bit of a bone shaker, but to a boy's mind it could be a classy car or a truck

Peerie Pheelie and Lowrie.

or even a Bren gun carrier – anything but a barrow.

One Monday after my usual glass of milk and sandwich, Mrs Horne said, "I have some eggs to go to the shop, will you manage them?" Fortified by milk and bread, I said, "Oh easy, I can do that no bother." I got the basket tied on the barrow and Mrs Horne came with a full size biscuit tin and set it in the basket. She said, "There are eight dozen eggs in the tin, so you will be careful."

I was very careful all the way out the Horne's road. However, when I reached the Short Scord I somehow forgot all about the eggs and the barrow became a Bren gun carrier. Down the Short Scord I charged, up the Mill Brae, past the school, down the New Road, along the Main Street and on to the shop. Up the two steps into the shop, along the shop floor, then up five steps to the back shop. As I was going up the five steps, Carrie passed by and said, "Boy, what is yon yellow stuff running out of yon box."

Mrs Horne milking, 1930s.   © C.J.W.

My heart just about stopped. Oh no, the eggs! I went into the back shop and quickly got the box open. I stared in dismay at the contents. Each egg had been wrapped in newspaper and now broken eggshells and bits of newspaper were all floating in a most revolting mess. I went to the top of the steps and seeing Chrissie, beckoned to her, "Come and see this." "What is it?" she asked. "I'm broken some eggs, come and look," I whispered. She took a quick glance and said, "Go and fetch Lolly".

Lolly was outside serving a customer at the petrol pump, so I went over and told him, "I'm broken some eggs and Chrissie says you are to

Mrs Horne and son George stooking corn, 1930s.   © C.J.W.

come and look." "Oh dear," he said. "All right, finish giving this car petrol." After the car went away I just stood by the pump, being too frightened to go back to the shop. What would Lolly say? What would Lolly do? At the very least, I would get the sack. There would be no more work at Nicolson & Co.

Then my thoughts were interrupted by Lolly's voice, "Willie, come here." He was standing on the pavement outside the shop with the biscuit tin in his hand. I ran up the brae and he handed me the box, admonishing me with the words "Go and empty that in the sea and be a bit more careful next time." That was all he said, he never mentioned eggs again.

Chrissie had salvaged the remaining whole eggs and washed them. She offered to pay for the broken eggs, but Lolly would not hear of it. "It's just unfortunate," he said. I broke four and a half dozen eggs that day, which in wartime was almost an act of treason. Needless to say, I never had eggs as cargo on the Bren gun carrier again.

My Granny

My Granny at Ladysmith was, I suppose you could say, my confidant. In my young years I visited her most days and in the school holidays,

Granny, Bertha with John, me and my mother, Elizabeth, 1930.

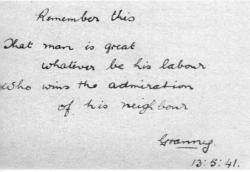

Remember this

That man is great
whatever be his labour
who wins the admiration
of his neighbour

Granny.

13: 5: 41.

Granny's writing.

every day. I was always talking and she mostly just listened putting in a word when it was needed. When I look back I think she was the most patient woman anyone could know. She baited haddock lines in the house and if I went along to ask for a drink of milk or water, or loaf and jam, she never said, "Run away and play, I will get it when I have finished this line." Granny never ever said no.

The Bus Boys

The Shetland Bus operations started at Lunna. However, needing somewhere to repair and service their boats, they later moved their operations to Scalloway. One day a group of naval officers headed by an admiral from Scapa Flow arrived at William Moore & Sons' smiddy. After a good look round, they told Jack Moore (who was boss) they would like to use the premises for repairs to Norwegian boats. Jack agreed, so this gave the Shetland Bus gang a safe west facing harbour with a Royal Artillery battery at the harbour entrance. They also had access to a readymade workshop in the marine engineering firm of William Moore & Sons.

Lunna Pier and House.   © C.J.W.

Further to the Norwegians' requirements was the Lord's Well beach (so called for the fine spring at the top of the beach) next to the workshop, where they could build a slipway for hauling up their boats.

The completed Prince Olav slipway awaits its first boat. From the right on the roadway are: 1st Inga Roald, 4th John William Slater; 5th myself; 6th Davie Fullerton, 8th Olaf Otterson; 13th Cissy Slater, 14th Pearl Mouatt, 16th William Duncan. Standng at the steps is Cecil Duncan. The two men at the rails are David Howarth and Ingvald Eidsheim.   *With kind permission of Sunnmøre Museum*

William Moore (we called him Mr Moore), originally from Orkney, was a blacksmith to trade. The firm did all kinds of smiddy work and also work for the fishing fleet. Now with the war they were working for the admiralty as well. The smiddy personnel at that time were Mr Moore and his two sons, Jack and Bob, Jamsie Thomson, Jimmy Leask, Loll Anderson and Cecil Duncan, an apprentice. Soon there were another two apprentices, Hugh Hughson and John Williamson, then later David Nicolson.

Heland, 2002.   © *W.S.*

Nell, Jack and Anna, 1943. Courtesy of Nell

When the Norwegians arrived from Lunna, engineers worked alongside the smiddy men. I can only remember the names of three engineers, Johan (Johnny) Haldorsen, Harold Angeltveit and Andreas Faerøy.

My sister Anna, newly left school, had started with the firm as a clerkess. Her office was a very small room in a corner of the workshop. She told of a very embarrassing moment when one morning Jack, who was talking to engineer Johan Haldorsen called to her as she came in the workshop and said, "Anna, Johnny wants a smoorikin," (the Shetland word for a kiss). Very red in the face she fled for the office and to her dismay saw they were following her.

In the office was a shelf where new tools and tools used only occasionally were kept. Johan reached up to the shelf, "Anna, this is what we call a smorre kann," he said as he lifted down an oilcan with a long spout. Then there was laughter all round.

Myself and Andreas Faerøy, June 2003.   Photo by Keith Morrison

The work load in the office had increased rapidly, so part of the deal with the navy was that Jack's sister-in-law, Helen Smith (Nell), who came from Findochty, was released from the war work she was doing to come north to work with Anna in the office.

One day two Norwegians, Per Blystad and Arne Melkevik, appeared in Scalloway. Locally they became known as Pete and Nipen. They had a small motorboat. Much has been written elsewhere about them. Nipen married a local girl and a grand-daughter of their's is married and stays in Trondra. Soon now there were Norwegians everywhere. Work started to build the Prince Olav Slipway on the Lord's Well Beach.

A Royal Navy Lieutenant, David Howarth, who was in charge of the Norwegian operations at Lunna, was soon a familiar figure walking around Scalloway. One day I was outside Nicolson's shop when Lieutenant Howarth left the smiddy and walked along the street. A white spot was visible against his dark navy uniform; a hole in the heel of one of his black socks. Two women were also standing outside the shop and one turned to the other and said, "Whit yun man is needing is a wife."

Johan Haldorsen, engineer.
© *C.J.W.*

Well, in due course he got himself a Shetland wife, a lovely girl called Nanette Smith. One summer day in 1944 Lieutenant Howarth made a trip to Foula in one of the subchasers. There he met Nanette, daughter of Lizzie and Willie Smith, who lived at the Schoolhouse, Lizzie being at that time the Foula teacher. Romance blossomed between David and Nanette. That same year, on 28th December, they were married in the Sandness kirk, on the Shetland mainland, where the Smith family had moved. Nanette told me that some of the Bus boys formed a guard of honour outside the church. She also said that the photographer never turned up, so they had no wedding photo until some weeks later, when they visited Clement Williamson's studio in Scalloway.

The Netloft at Westshore was taken

David and Nanette Howarth.
© *C.J.W.*

The three cooks: Albertsen, Holmlund and Ottersen.
Courtesy of Georgie Duthie.

over for the Norwegians and the village people soon renamed it Norway House. A name it still has today. The ground floor was used as a store; the first floor had the cook house and dining room. The loft was sleeping quarters. There were two cooks I remember the names of, Albert Albertsen and Olaf Ottersen. The cook on the *Hitra* was Holmlund, Swedish by birth and married to a Norwegian lady. When the *Hitra* was in Scalloway he worked at Norway House, as did Inga Roald. If we were in Norway House we would get a cup of coffee, which I must admit smelled much better than it tasted. The coffee pot was stewing on the fire all the time, so it was very strong, especially on a palate used to Camp coffee out of a bottle.

At the same time two Nissen huts for sleeping quarters were built opposite Lowrie Williamson's kiln. The huts were about three or four feet apart. Everybody had a hatred of Hitler and the Germans, but Pete's hatred seemed to be more intense than anyone else's. One day John (my cousin) and I found Pete painting a full size picture of Hitler on a wooden frame. "Whit's du gyaan tae du wi yun?" we asked. "Shoot Hitler," was the reply. When Hitler was finished, Pete set him up at the far end of the opening between the

ssen huts at Norway House.

Per Blystad.   *With kind permission of Sunnmøre Museum*

huts. Then, signing for us to stand aside, he stuck his revolver in the waistband of his trousers and walked (as Corporal Jones from Dad's Army would say), nonchalantly past the near opening. On seeing Hitler he would pull the revolver, wheel to the left and shoot until the gun was empty. Then he would go to see how many mortal wounds Hitler had sustained. We, of course, ran with him crying, "Look dere's een, hey dere's anidder een." Bullets flew thick and fast for days. Fortunately the only one who got punctured was Hitler.

One day John George Nicolson was walking down Hillside Road (or as it was known then, the Wast Back Road), when he heard shots coming from the direction of the Nissen huts. Looking over the dyke into the park, he saw Pete firing a pistol and a tin jump after each shot. The Luger was now empty, and as Pete reloaded John went over the dyke and ran to the tin. It was full of holes and as he picked it up some red and sticky liquid ran over his fingers. It startled him for a moment, until he realised it was strawberry jam. John congratulated Pete on his good shooting. Pete's reply was, "Pity it was not bloody German."

Prince Olav Slipway and Howarth's boatyard, 1950s.　　　© *C.J.W.*

John and I kept a careful eye on the building of the Prince Olav Slipway on the Lord's Well beach, visited by Crown Prince Olav on 14th October, 1942. The lower floor of the weaving shed was taken over for the Norwegians and the winch and engine for the slip were installed there. The rest of the area was used as a carpenter's workshop.

One day after school I went to check how the engine was getting on. There were six Norwegians crowded around it so I edged a bit closer. One man had lit a huge blowlamp on the top of the engine to warm up the cylinder head. A rope was put around the flywheel and there were two men on every side holding the rope. I crept even closer. The engineer, Harold Angeltveit, raised his arm, the men at the flywheel started to pull the rope, first one side, then the other and so on. When Harold dropped his arm, two of the men gave an extra hard pull and at the same time Harold pushed over a lever, the other man stopped the blowlamp, and with one almighty bang the single cylinder engine sprang into life, with a tonk tonk sound just like the fishing boats.

To say I got a fright would be putting it very mildly. My feet were inches off the floor. Then the men all clapped each other on the back and as I was in among them I got a few claps as well. When Harold was across in 1987 at the *Hitra*'s first return visit we talked about that day and had a laugh.

With the engine now fully operational, soon the winch and everything else was all connected up and the first boats were hauled out of the water. Everything went well until they tried to slip a larger boat, the *Andholmen*. She was much too heavy and only got half way up when something carried away and the cradle with the *Andholmen* headed back for the sea. The *Andholmen* floated off and the cradle went off the end of the rails. However repairs were soon done and with double pulleys and the wire rope fixed to the cradle all was well. The slip still works today, but not with that old tonk tonk engine

The Royal Hotel, West Shore (later to be The Walter and Joan Gray Eventide Home), was used to billet Norwegians before Norway House was ready, and also ME7 personnel.

The proprietor of the hotel was Willie Blance. The back door of the hotel opened on to Kirk Park and there was a long passage with a concrete floor, which led to the kitchen. In the wintertime this was the hotel entrance. It was a time of ·snow and when the men came in they would stamp their feet

Royal Hotel and Seaview House. © *C.J.W.*

to get the snow off their boots. When the snow thawed this of course left little puddles on the floor. Willie Blance was going out one day as some Norwegians were coming in, stamping their feet. He pointed to the puddles and said jokingly, "You boys piss on the floor?" Those who understood laughed, but one Norwegian's English did not include the word piss, so he asked one of the others to explain and was just referred to the puddles of water on the floor.

A little way along Main Street there was a shop and behind the counter was Mary, a nice, young and attractive girl. Soldiers and Norwegian sailors would make errands to the shop just to chat to her. It was winter and cold, so as there was a fireplace she always had a good fire going. This also attracted people as the little shop was warm. Coal dust or dross was available, and if water was added to this, mixed, and laid on hot coals it would cake over and the fire would lie on for a long while.

On this particular day after being in the hotel the Norwegian boys had wandered over to the shop. The fire was burning bright and Mary thought it was time to put some coal dust on. She got the bucket of dust and poured in water from a kettle. She gave it a good mix and as she was about to put it on the fire, the English learning Norwegian thought it time to try out some new words. Very proudly he said, "You piss in coal Mary?" Mary gave him a shocked look. After much laughter from the boys and a proper explanation, a very red faced young Norwegian left the shop in a hurry.

Alice Forsyth stayed in Seaview House on Main Street and rented out two rooms for a time in 1943 to Henry Nilsen, his wife and two children. Also staying at Seaview were two soldiers attached to ME7; Stanley Dobson and Bunny House. Dobson worked at Dinapore and House at the Scalloway Hotel. Henry Nilsen, I think, worked at Norway House.

A Norwegian in Scalloway some years after the war met Lexie Watt near Seaview and asked about the old lady who used to stay there and about Mrs Nilsen. Lexie was just the right person ask as the old lady, Alice, was Lexie's grandmother.

They spoke about the war days and he told Lexie that one day he was walking along the street when he saw Mrs Nilsen and the old lady talking and laughing together. He said he was shocked because he knew that Mrs Nilsen could

Scalloway Hotel.   © C.J.W.

not speak English and this old lady must be talking Norwegian. This really worried him, as he thought that someone could perhaps hear what Norwegians might be saying to one another about Bus operations as they walked along the street. They would never be thinking anyone in Scalloway could understand Norwegian. He decided to walk as near to them as he could so as to hear what they were saying. What he heard almost made him laugh out loud. Mrs Nilsen was talking about a milking cow they had back home in Norway and the old lady was talking about the weather. Neither knew what the other was saying but they were enjoying their conversation together.

Adie's weaving shed was at street level and below was the Norwegians' carpenters' shop and the slipway engine. The male weavers had been called up for military service so local women and young girls were trained to weave the tweed. The weaving looms were always positioned so that, as far as possible, the weavers sat with their backs to a window. This was so the light would be directed on to the woven tweed. The windows on the seaward side of the building overlooked the slipway and the yard where there were always Norwegians present, so the girls got lots of whistles.

One day Rolf Nordhus threw some shingle at one of the windows and a stone broke one of the panes. Mary Jamieson, the lady in charge of the weaving shed, was very annoyed and told the girls she would soon sort out these Norwegians. She stormed into the carpenters' shop and told all there, in no uncertain terms, to get the window repaired at once. The man in charge said he was sorry this had happened and he would send Rolf to effect repairs. Rolf, always cheery and laughing, fitted a new pane of glass and by the time he was finished he and Mary were the best of friends.

The electricity for Scalloway was supplied by H. Williamson & Sons, who provided 100 volts DC current for the east side, and by W. Moore & Sons, who supplied 110 volts DC current for the west side of the village. At that time wireless sets needed three batteries; a dry battery, a grid bias battery and an accumulator. This last battery, also known as "da weet battery", was made of clear glass. It had two terminals on top, was full of lead plates and some sort of acid liquid and had a frame handle. This accumulator could be recharged, while the other two could have a little longer life if warmed on the top of the stove!

H. Williamson & Sons was known as Harry's and W. Moore & Sons was known as Moore's. Both firms had battery charging stations. When a wireless gave up it was usually the accumulator. Most people had two accumulators. If they got their electricity from Harry's they went there with their weet battery. Alternatively, if they were a Moore's customer that was where they went. The dud battery was handed in, they paid a shilling and (hopefully), they were given a battery that was fully charged.

One day a gentleman from the country arrived at the top of Moore's road on his cycle. He was a harmless, absent minded, school teacher's husband. Leaning his cycle against the dyke, he untied his accumulator from the cycle carrier and made his way to the smiddy. After paying a shilling and getting his replacement weet battery, he walked up the smiddy brae towards his cycle. As he was about to fix the battery to the carrier he decided to look and see what was in it, and presumably to see what he had paid his shilling for. He lifted the battery to eye level and was peering into it when two Norwegians saw him.

As he was facing towards Moore's pier they thought he was taking photos of the boats. They ran up the brae, grabbed the spy, one on either side, and ran him down the brae and into their office. Jack Moore was in the smiddy when he heard men running and was just in time to

Norwegian boats at Nicolson's Pier. Norway house on the right. Post war. © *C.J.W.*

Fishing boats at Nicolson's Pier, reminiscent of wartime, 1950s. © C.J.W.

see the school teacher's husband, still carrying the weet battery, being half carried into the Norwegian office. Not knowing the circumstances, but hardly able to keep a straight face, Jack hurried across to the office. The sailors were both talking to the officer and he was seriously listening to them, when he saw Jack come in the door laughing. The

Nicolson's Pier. © C.J.W.

officer held up his hand for quiet and waited for Jack to speak. Jack pushed the sailors aside and explained about the accumulator. The officer explained to the sailors and they straightened the old man's jacket which had become a bit ruffled. The officer apologised and Jack helped the old man with his accumulator up the brae and back to his cycle.

As I said earlier, Uncle Robbie rented part of Adies store for a spare time workshop. With more work being done for the military, my brother's firm had grown and the workshop opposite William Moore and Sons was now not large enough. More workshop space was needed, so Uncle Robbie, who worked for my brother's firm, gave up his workshop for the duration of the war. The Shetland Bus people had moved next door. Their store man was a Norwegian called Jansen and he and Uncle Robbie became great friends. Uncle had a son, John, a prisoner of war in Germany, so Jansen and Uncle Robbie had a common hatred of the Germans.

When I started work in my brother's firm, most of my early time was spent with Uncle Robbie in the workshop. Jansen would visit nearly every day and always offered and gave Uncle Robbie a cigarette. This caused me great amusement as Uncle Robbie was a pipe smoker and he had a large moustache. He used to purse and pout his lips as far out as possible, then carefully insert the cigarette. Jansen would light a match and hold it towards Uncle Robbie. How I managed not to laugh out loud I do not know. As soon as the cigarette was alight, out of his mouth it came. He got three or maybe four puffs before it burned away. One day the cigarettes were about half through when someone called Jansen and he had to go. Uncle stubbed out his cigarette and said, "Dem dis fags." (A polite swear word.) I remarked that he should refuse them. "Min I canna do dat, hit wid be unfriendly." So Uncle Robbie's discomfiture and my amusement continued.

At the war's end Jansen, who was clearing up the store, came in one day and gave the two of us trousers and shoes and other odds and ends. My trousers and shoes fitted perfectly, so I was delighted. I put the shoes on next day to work. When Peerie Jeck came in the shop for nails he said, "Dir an awful smell o new shoes here Robbie." After some laughing, Jeck said to me, "Boy go home and get an old pair of shoes on an keep yon eens for Sunday." I looked at Uncle Robbie, and he said, "I wid say dat." So that's what I did, kept them for Sunday.

The Norwegians had four small boats – three Shetland models and one with a square stern that had come across from Norway. (At the war's end Bertie Burgess bought this boat.) They used these boats to go off to the Shetland Bus fleet of fishing boats lying at anchor in the harbour. Later they had Shetland models, built by Walter Duncan, on the subchasers.

One day, I don't remember which year, at the first of the school summer holidays, John and I were at a loose end. What were we going to do? John suggested that we go and ask the Norwegians for a smaa boat. We went to their office, which was opposite Moore's smiddy and knocked on the door. A voice inside called, "Come." In we went and John asked, "Can we get a len o a smaa boat." The officer smiled, "Ah dey lettle boys want a boat huh, OK, come with me."

Off we went to where the boats were tied between two slopes. He pointed to one of the Shetland boats and said, "Take that one." So we let go the ropes and got aboard and rowed away. He stood and watched us till we were a good bit from the pier, checking that we could handle a boat.

John was good at handling a boat, much better than I was We got the boat day after day, and rowed around the harbour and East Voe, but never out past the Royal Artillery battery at Port Arthur. We made a sail out of hessian sacks and fixed the sail to an oar. We rowed up wind across the harbour, then propped the oar with sail in the bow and sailed down wind. Back and fore we went, it was good fun.

One day one of the Shetland boats was missing and we wondered where it had gone. Visiting the Norwegian's carpenters' shop

Sevrin and Inga Roald, owner of Heland. © C.J.W.

later, we found it there. What was wrong with the boat we wanted to know? One of the carpenters said, "We fit motor." And they did. I understand it was the first one and half horsepower Stuart Turner engine in Shetland.

No one realised at that moment in time just how popular these engines were to become in post war Shetland. A whole new way of life was opened up for men with small boats. They went with their families to the outer isles and went fishing for lobsters along the shores. But that's another story.

Once the engine was fitted the boat was back between the slopes. Whenever we asked for a boat, the lieutenant always came with us and would point to which boat we were to take. Coming back with the boat on one occasion we saw a Norwegian slipping the ropes of the motorboat. "Whars du gyaan?" we asked. "Go to pump boat," he said, so we promptly asked if we could come with him. "Come onboard," he said, so we did. Once out past the crabbie lines he started the motor. What a thrill it was, our first time in a motorboat and what a speed it seemed to go. When we came to one of the Shetland Bus boats he helped us aboard. While he pumped, we explored all over the boat. We saw two big oil drums on deck, which we knew covered the machine gun placements, and lots of other exciting things. Soon he called us and we were back in the smaa boat with the motor purring away. He then took us for a tour of the harbour. It was all very exciting.

A few days later we went to the office as usual to ask for a boat (we never took a boat without permission). When we got to the slopes, John asked the lieutenant if we could get the motorboat. "No, no, no, you take that one there," he said. He watched us rowing away for a moment or two as usual then disappeared. "Right," said John, "back in and get the motor boat. I can work the engine." We were going to be bad boys. While I had been enjoying the motor boat run to the fishing boat with the Norwegian, John had been watching how he started and operated the engine; switch on petrol, tickle carburettor, a half turn with the starting handle, there was nothing to it. So we rowed back in, tied up our boat and let go the ropes on the motorboat. While I rowed out past the crabbie lines John shipped the rudder, then started the motor and we were away. We smiled at each other; what excitement, it was great, this was the life. However, the officer had not gone back in the office as we expected, but was talking to someone when he heard the motor start.

He thought he had better check who was taking the motorboat. When he saw the two little boys he waved his arms about. As I was sitting facing the stern of the boat I saw the officer and signalled to John and pointed. John looked over his shoulder, turned the boat, cut the motor and we went back in. In silence we tied up the boat, fearful at what the officer would say. Looking back on the incident I think he was highly amused. However he said, "You bloody bad boys. You go home now. You get no more boat. Go." We went up the road very deflated. It was indeed a disaster, no more rowing and sailing. What a terrible thought.

We kicked our heels for about a week, then knocked again on the office door. The usual shout, "Come." When we went in the officer said, "Ah, its the bloody bad boys and they want a boat, huh." Silently we both nodded. "OK, but no more in motor boat, huh. Come." We got a boat and what bliss it was to be back rowing and sailing.

When the three subchasers, *Hessa*, *Vigra*, and *Hitra* arrived in Scalloway, we thought they were huge boats. But when we saw *Hitra* lying alongside Blackness Pier in 1987 she did not look big compared with the modern Shetland fishing boats.

The Norwegians never seemed to mind John and I climbing over their boats. One day, on the *Hitra*, one of the older Norwegian men signalled us to climb on the seats which were on either side of the Bofors anti-aircraft gun. There were two handles like cycle pedals and he signalled us to turn them. One handle turned the gun barrel up and down, the other from side to side. We soon got the hang of it, and every now and then we would shout, "BANG, BANG, another German plane down." The Norwegian obviously thought it a great fun as he was smiling as he stepped ashore. No one ever chased us away or told us to leave the guns alone. Sometimes of course the barrel of the Bofors would be clipped down and we did not get to play.

A salute from Hitra leaving Scalloway, 2001.
© W.S.

A girl became pregnant and as she was friendly with a Bus boy it was assumed he was the father. After the baby was born, the following conversation by three elderly ladies was heard. First lady: "Lasses, Babs' bairn is been born." Second lady: "Yeah, I heard it was a bonnie ting." Third lady: "Poor ting, I feel awful sorry for it." First lady: "What on earth for, Babs is a fine strong lass." Second lady: "Poor ting indeed, the bairn will be well looked after." Third lady: "No, no, that's not it. You see nobody will know what the poor bairn is saying." First lady: "For goodness sake, how do you make that out?" Third lady: "Well you see the bairn will be speaking Norwegian like its father."

When the restored *Hitra*, accompanied by Norwegian torpedo boats, came for a visit in 1987 it was the *Hitra* coming home to Scalloway, as she had done many times during the dark days of war. The British boat *HMS Shetland* was also alongside Blacksness pier.

My next door neighbour, Cecil Duncan, and I went to have a look at the ships, especially *Hitra*. When we went on board the guard gave us a very smart salute. Cecil was particularly interested in the engines as he had worked at Moore's during the war. After giving *Hitra*, especially the engine room with its original engine, a thorough going over we went aboard one of the torpedo boats. We were all over it as well, but once again it was the engine room and the

Cecil in Hitra's engine room, 1987.   © W.S.

Willie at Hitra's ack ack gun, 2001.
© W.C.T.S.

Three veterans: Kaare Iversen, Albert Eilertsen and Rolf Nordhus.
Courtesy of Marina Gray

massive engines it contained, that interested Cecil. After a good look round we went to the wheelhouse, or control room, and I sat in the coxswain's seat. Then it was back to the *Hitra*.

A small Shetland model boat was fixed at the stern of the *Hitra*. As Cecil and I stood and looked at it, Wilbert Fullerton came up to us and said, "Du you tink dis is een o Walter's making?" Walter was Walter Duncan, boat builder from Hamnavoe; Cecil's uncle, who in the wartime had built three small boats for the subchasers. Cecil replied, "If I could see da honeyspot I wid ken."

The boat had a shaped canvas cover and it was lashed down, all very shipshape and Bristol fashion. Wilbert set about easing off the canvas at the bow, we all looked, and Cecil said, "Yes, its one of Walter's making." So it was one of the original wartime boats. Wilbert then put the canvas back and fastened the lashings. No one said anything to us in all our explorations. So Cecil and I went ashore well pleased with our reunion with the *Hitra*.

We thought we would visit the British boat, *HMS Shetland*, but guess what? They would not let us aboard. "No visitors allowed," said the guard. Two Shetland men crawled all over two Norwegian Navy boats, but were not allowed aboard a British boat. We concluded that the

Norwegian Navy trusted the Shetlanders, but the British Navy, well, perhaps not.

We knew all the fishing boats the Norwegians had and would soon notice when one was missing from anchor. Some days later the boat would be back, sometimes with a small fir tree tied to the mast head and we would then speculate as to what they had been doing, and where. One day a story went round the village that one of the boats was lost. All highly secret you understand, but we all knew it was the *Bergholm* with Larsen as skipper.

People wondered and worried what had become of the *Bergholm*, Skipper Leif Larsen and his crew, as several kent faces were not to be seen round the shore. Larsen's engineer, Bjornoy was in hospital in Sweden (although we did not know it at that time) so Andreas Faerøy (a visitor to our house) was asked to go in his place. It is well documented in David Howarth's book *The Shetland Bus* that the *Bergholm* was attacked and sunk by German planes off the coast of Norway. All the crew, but one, reached Norway in their small boat and were hidden and looked after by friends until an M.T.B. could be sent from Lerwick to fetch them. I was in Nicolson's shop one day when I saw a Norwegian going limping along the road. When I saw it was Andreas I had to run and speak to him. The Shetland Bus men were part of the village. They visited people's houses and were made to feel at home, just as lots of soldiers were. They would be affectionately referred to as so and so's Norske.

The *Brattholm* was a fine strong seventy-five footer, one of the larger boats, and was having her single cylinder engine overhauled. When it seemed to be running fine with a good tonk tonk it was decided to have a run out around the isles. This was to take place on a Sunday afternoon. Jon Haldorsen went to Moore's office and said to Anna and Nell, "Sunday, we hope is going to be nice day. We go for a run with the *Brattholm* to test the engine, so we invite you to come with us." They were at a complete loss for words. What would their folk say? What would the boss say? What would the villagers say? As the two of them went to church on Sunday, what would the minister say? Two lasses, going on a boat with Norwegians. Goodness me, and on a Sunday too.

Anna and Nell conferred and decided that if Jon was so kind as to ask them, then why should they not go. They would enjoy the run on the boat, and folk, well they could think what they liked. Sunday was indeed a fine day and they had a fine run away westward among the isles, then out between the isles into the western ocean with the engine tonk tonking happily away. Coffee and biscuits were served and Anna and Nell did enjoy the run. No harm was done, but it gave folk something to speak about.

What nobody knew was, that the *Brattholm* was shortly to leave on a

Kaare meets the Queen. © *C.J.W.*

special mission to Norway, and neither the crew nor the *Brattholm* would ever see Scalloway again. It was a sad time for the Norwegians and for many houses in the village it was like a family bereavement.

One of the Bus boys, Rolf Nordhus, used to visit the Horne family of Blydoit. He said to Mrs Horne on one occasion, "I won't see you for some little time now," and with a twinkle in his eye asked, "anything you would like me to bring back for you?" As it was getting on for Christmas, she, with a twinkle in her eye said, "How about a Christmas tree?" About a week or so later she opened the door one morning and a six-foot Christmas tree fell in. Nobody asked, but everyone knew where it came from. Some other houses in the village got Christmas trees as well.

I suppose the Norwegian we knew best and longest was Kaare Iversen. He courted and married a neighbour, Cissie Slater. I smoked my first cigarette at their wedding. After the war they were in Norway for a time. Kaare told me of the struggle the Bus men had with the Norwegian government in trying to get

Kaare, Cissy and family. © *C.J.W.*

Birgar Igland, Arne Melkavik, Barbara Christie and Rosaline Sinclair. © *C.J.W.*

Molly's wedding, June 1945. Jorgen Jensen, Kolbjørn Kristiansen, Molly Watt and Maggie Hughson. © *C.J.W.*

Cissie's wedding, 6th December, 1944. ?, Kaare Iversen, Cissie Slater and Maggie Hughson. © *C.J.W.*

the same pension rights as the army, navy and air force people. Feeling very frustrated at one point Kaare said, "To hell with you, we go home to Shetland." And they did, moving back to Scalloway. Eventually the Bus men did get their pension. In later years I used to try and speak Norwegian to Kaare but invariably he would answer in English. "Is so bloody long," he said, "since I speak Norwegian."

Three local girls married Norwegians. Barbara Christie married Arne Melkavik, Molly Watt married Kolbjorn Kristiansen and Cissie Slater married Kaare Iversen,

Military Establishment No 7, or as it was better known, ME7, the operators of The Shetland Bus, had their headquarters in Dinapore House. Their armoury was based in a Nissen hut at the east side of the fish sheds at Blacksness. In there they worked with guns of all kinds, grenades, small bombs, mines and detonators.

Being small boys, we wandered in there as well. I only remember the names of two of the armourers, Sergeant Harry Bass and Corporal Jimmy James. I recall Harry Bass

Dinapore, 2002.

Double Bass! 1944.

saying, "In our line of work you can't make a mistake, cause if you do, it could well be your one and only. Mistakes, however small are not allowed." In peacetime Jimmy James was a locksmith, I don't know about Harry Bass.

Jimmy James told of an incident in the armoury. Willie Burnett's Scalloway Hotel was also used by the military and one of the soldiers who worked there was called Bunny House. Bunny had got into the habit of going to the armoury for his eleven o' clocks and always sat on a large packing case. As he was not very tall and the packing case was, he had to put his hands behind him and heave

Clement J. Williamson and Cpl. Jimmy James. © *Mary Williamson*

M.E.7 Operatives: Sgt. Maj. Sherwood seated left; Quartermaster (Q) back centre.
© *C.J.W.*

Sgt. Harry Bass, centre, with friends. © *C.J.W.*

himself up, always setting his mug of tea there first. Jimmy said one day they decided to put a small detonator under the packing case lid. When Bunny heaved himself up, the detonator went off with a bang and they were all ready to laugh. They had to wait for their laugh, Jimmy said, as it was a good five seconds before Bunny jumped.

Bunny used to visit Uncle Robbie in the workshop and have a yarn. One day we were making a coffin when Bunny appeared. When he saw the coffin he wheeled around and was out the door in a flash and away along the street. Uncle Robbie shouted after him, but Bunny was a superstitious little man and did not stop. After that he would peep round the door before coming in.

The armourers would sometimes go to the back of the buildings occupied by W. S. Uncles, a Glasgow firm of fishcurers. There they woudl test fire revolvers and machine pistols, and the bullets would ping and thump into the stone building. Sometimes Norwegians were with them, learning to operate the various guns. Folks would tell us to keep away from the armoury and their guns, but boys will be boys and we were right in there.

Ping Ping

There were times when unpleasantness reared its ugly head, like one night at Blacksness House. Two families stayed on the ground floor and two families on the first floor. An old lady stayed in the attic. It was a tenement house, which I knew well, as my sister and her husband stayed on the first floor. The outside door was never keyed.

In Scalloway at that time were RAF personnel, soldiers from different regiments, navy men and Norwegians. One morning between one and two o'clock the door was opened with a bang that woke everyone in the house. Two people could be heard fumbling and stumbling in the stairway. There was no soundproofing in the house, and in the still of night every little sound carried; everyone knew who snored and who did not. Two men could be heard talking and it was realised they were Norwegian and very drunk.

They knocked on doors and shouted, and as we say nowadays, put the inhabitants in a state of fear and alarm. They went up and down the stairs two or three times, stumbling and knocking on doors and walls. When it sounded as if the two had reached the foot of the stairs, both men on the first floor stepped out on the stair landing. Nothing much could be seen, but suddenly one of the men from the ground floor opened his door. Some light streamed out, and so did he, armed with a fire shovel. The two watchers from above could now plainly see the two intruders were in Norwegian uniform. The down stair tenant wasted no time and struck the nearest Norwegian twice at the side of the head. Ping, ping, went the fire shovel. Then he went back in and shut his door. Drunk as they were, the two Norwegians stumbled quickly outside.

On the first floor the two tenants opened the landing window and leaned out. The two outside were talking loudly, probably planning an all out assault on the house, when an authoritative voice shouted something in Norwegian. Out of the darkness down Blacksness brae, came the owner of the voice, who turned out to be a Norwegian officer. At that time the area opposite Blacksness House and all round the fish sheds had stacks of fish boxes. Into this maze the two drunks staggered and hid. The two tenants in the landing window were now, hailed by the officer. He wanted to know what was going on and they were quite happy to tell him.

Next day an identity parade was held on Blacksness Pier. However the three people who saw the two Norwegians said it was impossible to pick out anyone. After the assembled company was harangued by an officer, two men stepped forward. They left Shetland next day and an officer apologised to the people of Blacksness House. Good relations were restored all round.

Ringing the Changes

One night, two shop workers, Mary and Joan, met on the street. They chatted for a while, then Mary said, "My, I was embarrassed on Wednesday. A soldier came in the shop and bought a packet of fags, and gave me what I thought was a two shilling piece. When I gave him his change he said, "Excuse me, but that was a half crown I gave you. I had to go to the till and get a sixpence for him. Was my face red?" "That's odd," said Joan. "The same thing happened to me on Wednesday, so I know how you felt."

A few nights later Joan met Agnes, also a shop assistant. During their girlie talk Joan recounted the story as told by Mary, and that it had also happened to her. To Joan's amazement, Agnes could claim the same happened to her on Wednesday. "What was the soldier like?" asked Agnes. "Well, he was good looking," answered Joan. "Tall, black hair, big eyebrows, but no smiles." "By jove," said Agnes, "that sounds like the same man. Funny we should all make the same mistake with him. I'm usually very careful with money."

The story now soon got around all the shops; watch out for a soldier paying with a florin and having to get change. The soldier tried his luck again, but this time it was a wily old shop owner who

Jamsie Williamson and Jim Manson.
© C.J.W.

took the soldier's two shilling piece. Magicians and con men are good at palming coins. However the shop owner was neither a magician nor a con man, but he palmed the soldier's florin with the ring finger of his left hand. Fetching change from the till, he laid it on the counter. "Excuse me," said the soldier, "but that was a half crown I gave you." The shop owner, Jamsie Williamson, from the corner shop at Blacksness, opened his left hand and said, "That is the coin you gave me, and son, if you ever try this trick in Scalloway again, you will be arrested. Now on your way." The soldier gathered up his change and made a hurried exit.

The Kitchen Dresser

One of the personnel of ME7 was Sergeant Major Sherwood, who stayed with his wife and two children in a house on the New Street. There was a shed in the garden across the road from the house and the Sergeant Major, who was a wood working enthusiast, fixed up a bench and made various things.

Sgt. Maj. and Mrs Sherwood and family., 1944.   © *C.J.W.*

An old lady who stayed close by had a great longing for a kitchen dresser on which to display her cups and plates. Most people had one, but not her. The S.M. got to hear about the longed for dresser through wifie talk, and immediately saw this as a great project. He went and took measurements, told the old lady she would soon have a dresser and got started. All his spare time was spent in the shed sawing, chiselling, glueing, nailing etc. Getting wood seemed to be no problem to him.

Soon everyone along the street, and probably the whole

village knew about the new piece of furniture. It was the talk of the time and the war was forgot about. When you passed the shed at night the S.M. could be heard busily knocking and sawing and there was good humoured banter from visitors. However, one of his visitors remarked, "Is it not a bit big to get in through the old lady's doorway." The S.M. dismissed this as nonsense. Had he not measured where the dresser would stand?

The day came for the launch and he got some army friends to give a lift, as the dresser had to go over a dyke. Over the dyke was no problem; across the road, no problem; but the doorway, there was a problem now. On entering the house you were faced with a partition and stairway. The old lady's part of the house and door was immediately to the left and there was no way the dresser could negotiate such a sharp turn. They pushed and they pulled, but to no avail. Someone laughed, the S.M. started to lose patience, and the dresser was quickly back across the road, over the dyke and safely in the shed, to the grins and delight of a crowd of onlookers. The S.M. then closed the shed door and worked away on his own, clear of spectators. The dresser was cut in two or maybe three pieces, then, with no spectators, carried quietly across the road and reassembled in the old lady's house. She was delighted, as all her cups and plates could now be on display. And the sergeant major got credit for a nice piece of work.

The Royal Visit

One day in the armourers' Nissen hut everything was swept clean and the place all spick and span. What was supposed to be a closely guarded secret was known all over the village. Crown Prince Olav of Norway was visiting Scalloway.

I was at Blacksness that day and

Slipway tablet. © C.J.W.

Prince Olav Slipway and carpenter shop. © C.J.W.

Andy in good style with May Stewart.
© C.J.W.

saw the Crown Prince go in the Nissen hut. Before arriving at the hut the Crown Prince had, at the other end of the village, unveiled a granite plaque at the slipway. The date was 14th October, 1942. Andy Irvine of Asta, in his red and blue essy kert got involved in the royal occasion. Andy tells that he was going west along the Main Street, collecting as he went, and on to Port Arthur and the Royal Artillery camp. He noticed quite a lot of staff cars and military personnel as he passed the Prince Olav slipway but you always saw that, so there seemed to be nothing unusual.

After being at the Port Arthur camp he came back to Main Street and joined in behind a grand parade of military vehicles, one of which, unknown to Andy, was carrying the Crown Prince of Norway. There were quite a variety of cars and they drove along Main Street very slowly. At the Burn Beach the convoy of cars, complete with Andy and the red and blue essy kert bringing up the rear, headed for Blacksness. Andy reckoned that not many people had ever had the privilege, or honour, to drive an essy kert as part of a royal procession.

Church of Scotland Canteen

The United Free church building, which was used for a school gym hall (now the Kirk Business Centre), was taken over as a Church of Scotland canteen. The ladies of the village were in attendance and provided cups of tea, cookies and buns for members of the military. Sometimes there would be concerts, and always a cup of tea at the interval. One night at a concert when tea was dispensed I remember Mary Jamieson say, "Na bairns, whit is dis? Shurly da lem wyshing up water."

My sister Anna told of one night, the 17th May it was, when two RAF boys came in late and they were very drunk. One of the ladies said she was surprised they were in such a state and got them to drink tea. After a little while one went out and was sick. When he came back in he said, "That's the last time I celebrate Norwegian Independence Day." They had met some Norwegians and had been in Norway House for a while of the evening and some heavy drinking.

Welcome Home

Nearing the war's end, we heard that prisoners of war were being marched deeper into Germany and letters from Johnnie and Davie ceased. These were difficult days for Uncle Robbie and Aunty Maggie, also for Jack Slater and his daughter, Nina. One wonders what went on in their minds in the quiet of the night. Speculation was rife, but the military had nothing to say. Some folk were full of woe, while others like uncle's other son Bob (Dobbel), were very cheery and said that the boys would soon be home.

Bob had made a flagpole, which he now set up on the top of Adie's quarry. Some thought it was a terrible thing to do with Johnnie and Davie missing, to be thinking of flying flags. Bob said, "When I hear that Johnnie is safe then I will hoist a flag and when folks see the flag flying they'll know too." From our kitchen window at Meadowfield we could see the flagpole. Whoever was up first in the morning – Chrissie, Anna or myself – the first thing we did was look out the window at the flagpole.

Passport photo list, 1945.

Gracie Fields' visit to the Shetland Garrison. © C.J.W.

Time passed, then one Sunday morning Anna looked out the window and there at the top of the pole a Union flag was flying. She came through the house shouting, "Johnnie is safe, Johnnie is safe, dir a flag fleeing." Chrissie and I had to get up and look at the flag; it was a great moment. After breakfast Anna and I went to Uncle Robbie's and confirmed that it was indeed true, Johnnie was in this country and would soon be home. Uncle Robbie and Aunty Maggie tried to look and act nonchalant but we all knew how they were feeling.

A few days later, uncle and I were working in the shop when we heard someone running down Adie's road. The shop had three steps up to the door. The footsteps stopped at the steps and a voice, which we both knew was Katrin Johnson, filled with excitement and emotion, shouted, "Robbie, Robbie, Robbie." Startled, we both ran to the door and Katrin said, "Robbie, Johnnie is in Lerwick and will soon be home." "Oh yes," said Uncle Robbie, "tanks tae dee lass." Katrin then turned and ran up the road to tell Aunty Maggie. The Johnson's were one of the few families at that time to have a telephone.

We went back to the bench in the shop, saying nothing. Uncle picked up his plane but his hands were shaking so much he had to put

Smith family, 1936. Chrissie, myself, Dad, Anna and Phyllis. © C.J.W.

it down. He looked at me and said, "I think I'll better go tae da hoose." And off he went.

Not long after, a car arrived and I saw John get out. After tea that night we went to the house to see Johnnie. A lot of people were in and there was much shaking of hands, and. "blyde tae see dee boy." When it was my turn to shake hands he said, "Boy du is fairly grown, du is nearly as big as me."

Later, Johnnie came to where I was sitting and asked with hand partly over his mouth, "Does du smoke?" I just nodded and he backhanded me a packet of American Lucky Strike cigarettes. It was great to see him home, and it was great to see Uncle Robbie and Aunty Maggie looking so pleased and contented after five years of uncertainty, heartache and worry.

It was about a week later that Molly Johnson rushed up to Myrtle Cottage with good news for Jack and Nina. Molly's brother Louis, had seen Davie in Lerwick. He was now, she said, at his Aunty Maggie's in Lerwick and Bob was coming with a car to take them to fetch him home. When they got to Scalloway all the neighbours were there to greet Davie. It was another emotional welcome home, a week after Johnnie's homecoming. For his father Jack, and his sister Nina, it must have been a great relief from the strain and worry they had had over the past five years.

So the war ended. Now my reminisce is over. I have just touched briefly, with the help of a lot of friends, on wartime stories in the village. There are lots of other tales still waiting to be told. This should be done now before they disappear with age and the passage of time.

CLEMENT

M y son, William, was a keen photographer and wanted to develop and print his own photos. When he bought an enlarger I fitted up a darkroom in the loft. One night, having found an interesting glass negative of Clement's I asked him to make a print of it. I recalled, when I was a young boy, being in Clement's darkroom while he and Mary were printing. Clement sat at the enlarger and Mary sat at the bench with the dishes of developer and fixer. If a large order was on then I stood in the middle, passing the cards from Clement to Mary. I only once recall doing any printing in The Studio, but that night, watching William printing from Clement's glass negative, it all came back to me. Clement's little tricks of the trade, his hands shading in parts of the picture, a little more light here, a touch there. It was an art, and he was an artist.

Before Clement left school, and for some time afterwards, he worked for Dr Bunty Yule, who stayed at Dinapore, where he also had his surgery. The doctor taught Clement a great deal about medicines. He also gave him medical books to read and Clement was very quick to learn. Clement did all sorts of jobs in and around Dinapore. At consulting time he would take the patients from the waiting room to the surgery.

One day, an elderly man came to see the doctor. When asked what was bothering him the old man replied, "Eh, what say you? I can't hear a word, I'm gone a bit deaf." So Dr Yule got his instrument for looking into ears and proceeded to look in both the old man's ears. He then asked Clement to heat some water and bring it into the surgery. Soon both ears were syringed and great lumps of wax and cotton wool came out. The doctor held up pieces of the cotton wool and showed it to the man. "No wonder you were deaf when you stuffed your ears with cotton wool. Clement, go and mix a Sedlitz Powder."

This powder was a powerful remedy for constipation, and it can have a very moving effect, depending on how far you are from a toilet. Clement was a bit puzzled, but did as he was told, mixing the powder and handing the glass to the doctor. Dr Yule in turn handed the glass to the elderly man and said, "Drink that now, as quick as you can." The old man drank up and thanking the doctor, left the surgery. When the last patient had gone, Clement said, "Doctor, I can't understand why you gave that old man a Sedlitz Powder because his ears were stuffed with cotton wool." The doctor gave Clement a knowing look and replied, "Silly old fool, it will give him something to think about."

Clement was very interested in flowers and had a small greenhouse built on the south side of his studio. He was particularly interested in liliums and had several varieties growing. At evening time when you walked along New Street the heady fragrance of the lilys would waft in the air, and in the greenhouse the scent was overpowering.

Clement was a well known raconteur and told stories to the many visitors to his studio. He told me about one occasion when he wanted to get a photo looking over the East Voe. One of the upper windows on the east side of the castle would, he thought, make a fine viewpoint. It was where there had been a staircase and was not very accessible. However, being a young man at the time, he climbed up no bother and leaned out of the window. This was not to his liking, so with the camera in his pocket he climbed into the window and sat with his legs outside. This, he said, was just right, and enabled him to take the photos he wanted.

It was a fine quiet evening with the sun far in the west and he sat in contemplation for a few moments. When he decided it was time to go, he discovered that, while it was easy to get into this situation, there was no way he could get down. What was he to do? It would be a while before anyone thought to come looking for him. It was no use shouting as there was no one to be seen. He sat there wondering what to do, when to his relief he saw a man coming rowing a boat up the voe. When the boat was just about opposite him, Clement shouted, "Hi." The man stopped rowing and looked shorewards. He saw no one, so started to row again. Clement shouted again, even louder. The man stopped rowing and shaded his eyes from the sun. Still he saw no one, so again commenced rowing. Clement all this time was waving an arm, and now shouted, "The castle, look at the castle." This time the man saw him and asked what he wanted. "Come and help me down, I'm stuck." The rower then came into the castle and, with much laughter, helped Clement down.

In the first year of the war, the upsurge of military personnel in and around Scalloway resulted in greatly increased business for Clement's studio portraiture. One day a clerk of works from the flying boat base

Clement and Thomasina Sinclair in The Studio door.

at Sullom arrived and asked him to come to the campsite and take passport photos. As Clement had as much work in The Studio as both he and Mary could handle, he felt disinclined to travel to Sullom. However, he had a licence or permit from the military to take photos in The Studio, and elsewhere when they required, so he agreed on condition that the clerk of works informed the security people at Sullom. Clement arranged to get a run to Sullom next morning with my brother Tammie. At the camp gate, Tammie was let through as he had a pass, but Clement was marched to the guard hut, and all his gear (cameras, box of glass plates, tripod, etc.) was confiscated and locked in a cupboard. The clerk of works had neglected to inform the security people.

When a security officer was called, he was adamant that there would be no photographs taken in or near the camp. The clerk of works was sent for. He told the officer it was official, that from two weeks yesterday all workmen had to have a photo passport or they would not be allowed into the campsite. "No photo passports, and you will be responsible for holding up the work."

"I know all that," said the officer, "but I am not having photos taken here." Clement had had enough. "Fetch all my cameras and gear, I'm going back to Scalloway. I'm not going to listen to any more fiddle faddle, I don't need your work, I have plenty to do in my studio," he declared. The officer jumped, "You can't do that. All right then, take the photos, with a Nissen hut wall as background."

So in groups of twenty, with some sitting on the grass, some sitting on chairs and with some standing, the photographing commenced. An RAF corporal policeman was there to watch every move. (At next day's photo session the policeman left at lunch time.) When the last photo was taken, Clement had to go to the RAF darkroom and develop the negatives. The darkroom was very well fitted up and Clement never understood why, with six RAF photographers there, the security people did not get them to take the passport photos. An officer had to come and look at the developed negatives, give them the OK, then destroy all the unused negatives, which grieved Clement sorely. Such was the way of security.

Back at The Studio, enlargements had to be made of all the groups of workmen. The passport photos had to be about one and half inches square. When the prints were all dried the enlargement was cut along the line of men, then, using a piece of glass the size of the finished product and a razor blade, the passports were produced. I can remember the work in The Studio. Two photos were produced for every man, and there were well over a hundred men.

The next group of men to be photographed were at Calback and there was no road there. The way to Calback was by an ex-fishing boat, skippered by a Lerwick man. Clement and the RAF corporal policeman stepped ashore and walked towards some huts. The first man they met was Robert Slater from Trondra, who was a contractor's foreman. He soon got a group of men together and Clement was setting up his tripod and camera when a hut door opened. Out came the man in charge, a naval captain, and he was furious. He called for Robert Slater and asked, "What the blazes is going on here?" "I go into my office for a cup of coffee, and when I come out the place is crawling with blooming photographers taking pictures everywhere." Then he saw the RAF policeman, "What are you doing here? This is a naval station, you are RAF; clear off at once." The policeman managed to get a word in, "These passport photos have to be taken." "I know that," the captain replied, "but why was I not informed? Well, get on with it."

When the photo session was finished, Clement discovered that the fishing boat would not be back until late, when the workmen finished for the day. He thought it was a bad job that he and the RAF corporal would have to wait around for hours. Then a naval commander appeared from one of the huts. "Hello Clement," he said, "I thought it was yourself." It was a Brae man. I think Clement said his name was Andrew Bigland. He was a master mariner, who had been in the merchant navy and had met Clement many years before in Scalloway. Anyway, in the ensuing conversation Clement complained about not being able to get back to Sullom. "We have a speedboat here," said Commander Bigland, "I will soon get you back to Sullom." He was as good as his word, and soon Clement was once more in the RAF darkroom developing his negatives.

The Letter

There were always visitors to The Studio, some from far and distant lands and speaking many different tongues. One day two people arrived, they were from France and could not speak much English. A man and his wife, she seemed to understand Clement speaking better than the husband did. They looked at photos, bought postcards and conversed for a while, then left. That would have seemed to be the end of them, but four weeks later a long letter arrived from the couple. It was written throughout in French, which Clement could not understand. He looked at it in some dismay then laid it aside, thinking maybe someday someone would visit who would be able to translate.

One day several weeks later, two middle aged ladies on holiday from the Edinburgh area came into The Studio. After general talk, then onto occupations, one of them said she was a school teacher. "Oh," said Clement, "what do you teach?" "I teach maths," was the reply. He looked at the other lady and said, "Are you a teacher as well?" "Yes," she replied, "I'm a language teacher, I teach French." "Oh," said Clement, "hold on a moment now, I'm going to show you a French letter." He realised by the shocked looks on both faces that he had made a boob, and they were probably thinking he was some kind of weirdo. He quickly hurried to his desk and much to the ladies' relief, came back waving the letter that had come all the way from France.

BUNTY

One spring evening in the early 1970s my son, who was a keen angler, asked me to drive him from our home in Scalloway to the Tingwall loch. I did so and told him I would be back about nine o'clock. Returning at approximately nine thirty, I tooted the horn at him as I drove north to turn at the boathouse. When I picked him up, he got in the van much more carefully than usual. I took notice, but said nothing. Just passing the standing stone, he said, "No troots Dad, but I got this," taking a dunter's egg out of his pocket. "What are you going to do with that?" I asked. "Hatch it out," was the reply.

At the house we found a small cardboard box and Mam tore up an old jumper, making a fine nest in which to place the egg. The box with jumper and egg was set on the hot water cylinder, which was in a cupboard off our bedroom.

As the days went past the egg was regularly looked at and everyone wondered if and when it would hatch. One morning I woke early and could hear a faint cheeping and tapping coming from the cylinder cupboard. I alerted the whole household and we carefully lifted out the box. Yes, the little dunter was there in the egg, tapping on the shell to get out and all the while cheep cheeping. What excitement there was during breakfast.

William set the box on a stool along a radiator in the kitchen and gave Mam orders to keep an eye on events. William and Kristine had of course to go to school. When I came home at lunchtime, Mam said she had helped the little dunter, as the shell was so hard it could not get out on its own. In nature the shell would be soft, but in the cylinder cupboard the constant heat had hardened the shell to such an extent that the poor little dunter would never have made it without her help. I looked in the box and saw a damp, pink little object with a large beak. I did not give it much chance of survival. However, with the heat from the radiator and Mam working away with an eyedropper and warm milk, by evening I thought, "Well, maybe you will make it." The bairns coming home from school were delighted with the new addition to the family and promptly named the little fellow Bunty.

As the days went past Bunty thrived, grew fine feathers and cheeped happily at everyone. Whether he thought we were all dunters or that he was human, we never knew, but that Bunty was part of the family was never in any doubt. He had the run of the house, but we always knew where he was by the excited cheeps. If we were all out during day or evening we tried to come into the house quietly on our return. What a welcome we got on opening the kitchen door. With loud cheeps he would come tumbling out of his box wanting someone to pick him up.

One evening a lady from New Zealand was visiting. She was holding Bunty in the crook of her arm – the crook of an arm was a favourite spot – when suddenly he climbed up and disappeared inside the neck of her loose fitting jumper. The lady thought it was a good

Kristine holding Bumty.   © *W.C.T.S.*

fun, and so did Bunty, obviously intent on becoming bosom friends. We all laughed and Bunty could be heard cheeping delightedly.

On occasion, William would fetch a spade from the shed and take Bunty over the hill dyke to look for live food. This was always a time of great excitement for Bunty. He would cheep happily, while greedily eating worms, beetles or anything else that was dug up. What a pity there were no camcorders then.

We took him to the beach one day thinking he would take to the water. But no, all he wanted to do was run along the beach behind us. After all, we were his family. We even tried him in the bath but he just did not seem to like the water. Sitting by the fire at night, Bunty would

Bunty pulls at Willie's trousers.   © W.C.T.S.

snuggle between your sock feet and cheep contentedly.

Bunty rapidly grew and his cheep was now changing to a quack. We still had lots of fun with him. He spent a lot of time on the back green where he would chase after me and tug and pull at my trouser legs. He never did this in the house, only outside.

We now realised that we could never let him go, because when outside he just ran to the first human he saw. Sadly, some humans are very cruel and do not treat birds or animals at all kindly. A decision had to be made. The bairns wanted of course to keep him, but what could we do over winter with a fully grown eider duck? A neighbour suggested a zoo. After much discussion the bairns agreed, and I wrote a letter to a Mr Leslie, Director of the Hazelhead Zoo in Aberdeen. I told all about Bunty and asked if there could be room for him at Hazelhead. Two weeks went past with no reply, then, late one night there was a phone call. It was Mr Leslie, he had just that day returned from holiday and would be delighted to take Bunty and give him a good home.

I made a wooden box with a wire netting front and one day we sorrowfully set off for Sumburgh Airport. Bunty quacked all the way. Arriving at Sumburgh we went to the British European Airways desk. I said to Jimmy Burgess, "We've got a young dunter here going to Hazelhead Zoo." He looked then said, "Man, that's going to cost dee a fiver." A fiver then, in the early seventies, was an awful lot of money. I said, "Well, if it has to be a fiver, then so be it." Jimmy said, "Go and see if you know anybody travelling to Aberdeen. If they say the dunter is their's, well, it'll only cost dee fifty pence." So leaving the family and Bunty at the desk, I went looking among the B.E.A. passengers.

There were some people I knew slightly, then I saw a man walking towards me, a man I knew, Peter Johnson of Roadside. "Peter, is du going to Aberdeen?" I asked. "Yes, yes," he replied. So I explained about Bunty and the fiver or fifty pence. "No bother at all," said Peter, and came with me to the desk and affirmed that Bunty was part of his luggage. I paid fifty pence.

When the cargo handler came and took Bunty it was a tearful farewell. In those days you could get near the aircraft, we went and watched Bunty in his crate being set in the cargo hold. For us it was a very quiet journey home, and no quack quack when we opened the kitchen door. That night we had a phone call from Mr Leslie. He had picked Bunty up at Dyce and he was fine. "I'm keeping him in the house tonight," he said, "just to keep an eye on him, then tomorrow he will go out in a pen. Can you hear him quacking? I'll give you a call in two weeks and tell you how things are." As promised he called, and told us that Bunty had settled in well and seemed quite happy.

There is no doubt that Bunty gave us all a lot of pleasure. I am sure that Bunty was very happy with us, but he was in the wrong environment. It is not something I would recommend anyone to do. We, and Bunty, were very lucky that Mr Leslie was willing to give him a home at Hazelhead Zoo.

LOWRIE'S

West Shore area showing Lowrie's kilns, centre, 1930s.   © C.J.W.

Hjaltland Housing's new development in Ladysmith Road, Scalloway has been very properly named Lowrie's, after Lowrie Williamson, who acquired the former kippering kiln in 1922. A lot of Scalloway people were employed at Lowrie's kiln over the years. At one time my grandmother, my mother and a sister all worked for Lowrie.

As a small boy, my friends and I often played in and around the rambling old building in the summer time. The building had been added to incrementally over time, and was full of stairs, storage rooms, smoke kilns and long dark passages. It was a fine and exciting place to play. We were always well mannered and of good behaviour; well, we had to be as most of us had sisters, mothers and grandmothers working there. Any unseemly conduct and we would have been banned, not I hasten to add by Lowrie, but by our own families.

Lowrie was a kind Christian gentleman and very tolerant of us young boys. We played outside where the women gutted herring for curing and split herring for kippers. We plied the cooper with questions like, "Whit's yon tool for?" and, "Whit's diss ene for?" We played in and around the corridors, up stairs, here, there and every-where, and nobody chased us. I don't think anyone ever had occasion to be angry with us. Lowrie would only ask, "Are you being good boys?"

The smell of herring being cured and the smell of the wood smoke and kip-pers, I think will always be with me. Looking back on life then, the weather always seemed to be fine. You never remember the rainy days when you had to play on the mat before the fire.

When I was six years old my father bought me a saw and clawhammer, thinking, I suppose, I would follow him into the joiner trade. After several saw marks in stools and chairs etc., the saw was laid up for a while. Then I only got to use it when supervised.

At the kiln us young boys wanted to make kipper

Jane Hunter and Chrissie Smith on left, others not known, 1920s. © C.J.W.

Jerry Watt, Hannah Mouatt, Mary Tulloch, Chrissie Smith, Bertha Umphray, ?, Jessie Moffat, Mymie Watt, ?, ?, Aggie Halcrow, ?, 1930s. © C.J.W.

Jamie Wishart on left, Lowrie right centre, 1930s. © C.J.W.

boxes. So we were given, in modern talk, a crash course on how it was done. The older hands could make a box in a flash; the sixteen nails went in like bullets. When you had made twelve boxes you got a penny, which was a useful sum of money for a young lad. Your boxes were all stacked together and when you had twelve you went and told Jamie Wishart Senior, the foreman. He came and

Herring curing at Port Arthur. Harry Cole, Charlotte Williamson, Jessie Slater and Babsie Paton, 1940s.

checked them over. If there were any that had a nail out the side, it was back to the bench. You lost time on this so it made you be careful.

Back row: Chrissie Smith, ?, Hannah Mouatt, Jessie Moffat, Aggie Halcrow, Mymie Watt. Front row: ?, ?, Mary Tulloch, Wilhelmina Duncan, ?, Bertha Umphray, 1930s. © C.J.W.

There were always orders for half boxes of kippers and at that time there was no saw at the kiln. Jamie Wishart would ask my sister Chrissie, who worked at the kiln, if he could borrow Willie's saw. The kipper box wood was all pre-cut except for making half boxes, where the end of a box was sawn in two. The sides and bottom were then nailed on, and there was a half box. Jamie always did the sawing himself.

After the half box orders were completed, Jamie would say to Chrissie, "Tell Willie to come for his saw." When I went to collect my saw, I would also be given a large bundle of kippers. We

Campbell Williamson and Len Laurenson.
© C.J.W.

then ate kippers for days afterwards; old fashioned fried kippers cooked on a number 7. No boil in the bag or tinned kippers then. The house stank of kippers and we smelled like kippers, but they tasted great and have never been equalled. I have no memories of winter time at the kiln, just of the herring season. It's mostly the good things that stick in your mind, and Lowrie's kippers were certainly good.

In 1957, while working in Burravoe, Hunter Sandison and I stayed with Magnie and Helen Johnson. Early one Thursday morning she asked if we could eat salt fish. We both said we liked salt fish, so at lunchtime a plate of salt whitings were on the table. After tasting a piece I declared that it came from Lowrie Williamson at Scalloway. Almost with disbelief, Helen asked, "How could you possibly know that?" I explained that Lowrie hung the salt fish in the kiln to dry them and lit a small fire, giving them a lightly smoked flavour. At that time, Lowrie sent salt fish on Wednesday, via the *Earl of Zetland*, to Mackie

After the fire.   © W.S.

Hughson at the Brough shop. The fish were so popular people had to place an order for them.

Alas, in the late 1940s there was an overnight fire which destroyed the whole complex; the wooden buildings burned like tinder. Next morning there was nothing left, the kiln and everything in it was razed to the ground. Lowrie, undaunted, set about building a new kiln and soon a fine building of bricks and concrete appeared. When Lowrie retired in the mid-sixties his family continued in business until the premises were vacated in 1987. Finally, Hjaltland bought the site and another part of old Scalloway disappeared. I'm so glad the name lives on; Lowrie's.

Lowrie and Mary with some of their family.   © C.J.W.

A GENTLEMAN CALLED JOHN L.

In the mid fifties, the firm of Thomas Smith and Son, Scalloway, built houses for Zetland County Council in the thriving community of Hamnavoe, Burra Isle. We, the workmen who stayed outwith Burra, travelled to and from Hamnavoe by M/B *Tirrick*, owned and operated by Hance Smith.

In the summer time it was a pleasant journey and always there were games of five hundred. On occasions

Hamnavoe in the 1950s.   © *C.J.W.*

there were tourists to chat to and, sometimes chat up. The winter though was a different story. It could be rough and not very fine. Sometimes we landed at Easter Dale and had to walk to the site at Hamnavoe. However, with Hancie and Andrew Henry we always felt very safe.

One new years eve, about ten to six, we left the building site to walk to the Hamnavoe pier to board the waiting *Tirrick*. Thinking we had

plenty of time I decided I would go via Highmount and wish my friends, John and Pheelie Sinclair a good new year. John and Pheelie were a very kindly couple and I had got to know them very well. It seemed I was in their house just a few minutes or so. When we came out it was with dismay that we saw the lights of the *Tirrick* well away from the

Ferry boat "'Tirrick".   © *C.J.W.*

119

M/B "Replenish".   © C.J.W.

Pier and heading full speed for Scalloway. I can not remember exactly what I said but it was not kindly disposed towards anyone on the *Tirrick*, that's for sure. "Never mind," said Pheelie, "Du'll just stay here wi wiss."

It was a fine night, very dark but folk were out about. A voice out of the darkness hailed us, "Whits happened?" "The *Tirrick* has gone and left me." I replied. "Well," the voice continued, "the *Replenish* is coming in to pick up men to gut and they are going to Scalloway so du wid win wi dem." Any other night, being left would not have bothered me at all, but it was new year's eve and there was first footing to be done. Just with that we saw the lights of the *Replenish* coming in by the lighthouse. So, saying goodbye to John and Pheelie, I set off for the pier with John's voice coming after me, "Mind noo dir a bed here for dee."

There were two or three men waiting on the pier. The *Replenish* came to the pier slowly and when her bow touched the men clambered aboard. I shouted to the crewman in the bow, "Are you going to Scalloway?" "No," he replied, "We are going to Easter Dale. Why?" My reply was brief, "The *Tirrick's* left me." By this time the boat was reversing from the pier. I turned away and started to walk up the pier back towards John and Pheelie's house, knowing that a welcome waited me.

John L. Pottinger, or John L,. as he better known, was skipper of the *Replenish* and now I heard his voice, "Whit wis yon man wanting?" The crewman answered, "Hit's een o da Scalloway men, da *Tirrick's* geen an left him." Next I heard VROOM from the engine and John L. say, "Shout on him and tell him tae come aboard." So the shouting was duly done and when the *Replenish's* bow touched the pier for the second time I clambered aboard. Again John L.'s voice, "Tell him tae come up in da wheelhouse." When I climbed into the wheelhouse he looked at me and said, "My mercy Willie, is hit dee dat da *Tirrick* is left, well boy we'll shune git dee tae Scalloway." I said, "You ken da wye o da *Tirrick*, men in da wheelhouse, men in da cabin and hit being dark I'm no surprised if someen gets left." We chatted for a while then he opened a window and called to Harry Laurenson, "Harry, string up some haddocks for Willie."

After a while Harry came into the wheelhouse with a large string of haddocks. As he laid them down he said, "Boy dis is going tae cost dee something, hire o a fishing boat tae Scalloway an a string o haddocks forbye." I was not very sure how to take this as Harry's face was unsmiling and so serious. Then he and John L. laughed together. Harry fairly enjoyed the joke and I suppose the look on my face.

The *Replenish* made her way to Scalloway and came in alongside Blacksness pier. It was with much thanks to John L. and the crew that I, with a large string of haddocks stepped ashore. I watched as the *Replenish* turned and steamed into the darkness of the harbour entrance and on to Easter Dale.

I made my way homewards and, on the last night of that year, we had fresh haddock fillets fried for supper. I often relate the occasion, and still give thanks to the crew of the *Replenish*, and a real gentleman, John L. Pottinger.

Crew of the "Replenish" in the 1950s. From left: Mike Jamieson, Harry Laurenson, Stanley Pottinger, John L. Pottinger (skipper), James Cumming, Malcolm Jamieson, Sam Pottinger, John William Pottinger.   *Photo courtesy of Keith Pottinger*

LOCKS

Icommenced my apprenticeship as a joiner with my brother's firm of Thomas Smith & Son in 1945 and soon became interested in locks and their workings. Old locks were often dumped, so I would take them apart to find out how they worked. Some were very simple and some more complex. I was helping Uncle Robbie in the workshop one day when a man came in carrying a paper bag. He emptied the bag out on a clear part of the bench, and out tumbled all the bits and pieces of a good quality rim lock. "It wasn't working," he said to Uncle Robbie, "so I took it off and it just fell to pieces. Will you put it together for me?" Uncle Robbie gave a one word answer – "Na." I had been ignored up to this point, but I was fascinated by all the levers, springs and other bits and pieces, so I said I would like to try. "Right," the man said, "I'm going to the bakeshop. I'll be back in about an hour."

I started to fiddle with the levers. Two were thin and one was a bit thicker, but in what order did they go? It was like a metal jigsaw puzzle. After a few minutes, Uncle Robbie gave me his advice; "Throw the dashed lot back in the bag, du's wasting dy time." Usually I did what Uncle Robbie said, but this time I was really interested and it was a challenge. I tried placing the levers in various permutations until they seemed to be in the right order, then the springs, by trial and error, were put into place. After some time everything seemed correct, so I screwed the back on and the lock worked like new. I laid it on the end of the bench and felt quite proud.

A while later the man came up the steps and into the workshop. "Well boy, did du get my lock fixed?" he asked. I pointed to the lock, but before I could proudly explain how I had repaired it he snatched it up, said, "Tanks tae dee, boy," and disappeared out the door. I must have looked a bit put out, because Uncle Robbie laughed and said, "Du'll learn. Du'll learn. Bit hits going tae be da hard wye, I doot."

Most houses and sheds at that time were fitted with rim locks and when one was renewed I always tried to get the old one for examination. One night I made a little tool that could open most rim locks. I used it on quite a few occasions whenever someone had lost their key. One day a man came into the shop and said to Uncle Robbie, "The key for my shed door is broken. Do you have any keys that might open the lock?" "Yes," said Uncle Robbie. "Go to the wast workshop. There are a few odd keys there and you might be lucky."

When he had gone I took my little tool, got on my cycle and went to the man's house. I climbed over the back fence and got to work on the shed door. After a few moments of fiddling and turning and twisting, clickety click the bolt slid back. I tried the handle and the door opened. I then closed it and set off back to the shop, thinking of the fun we would have with the man when I told him what I had done. When I told Uncle Robbie what I had done he was highly amused but said, "Now, not a word to anyone about this." "Will we no tell him?" I asked. "No, no, not a word." Half an hour later the man came in to return the keys. "Ken dis Robbie," he exclaimed, "whit a carry on. Da blooming shed door wis open aa da time." Uncle Robbie's face was a picture.

I was sixteen when I had my first encounter with a Yale lock or night latch or, as we called it, a jibb lock. An old lady who lived in an upstairs room in a house came in the workshop one day. Tammie and Geordie were working at one bench and I was at another. "Oh, Mr Smith," she said to Tammie, "I need to get a lock on my door. Du you ken, folk are coming into the house while I'm out." This they found hard to believe. "It has to be a jibb lock," she said as she went out the door. Tammie asked me if I had fitted a jibb lock before. I had not, but I felt sure that I could manage, so was assigned to do the job.

The lock came packaged in a box, together with instructions on how it was to be fitted. On the way to the old lady's house I got out the instructions and read them, so that it would look as if I knew what I was about. I fitted the lock then explained to the old lady how it worked and that she would have to remember to take the key with her when she went out, as the door was now self-locking. "Oh yes, yes, my dear. I'll certainly do that. Thank you kindly," she said.

When I got back to the shop, Tammie asked how I had managed. I said all had gone well. I had told the old lady all about the lock and to mind and take the key with her when she went out. I had hardly finished speaking when the door crashed open and the old lady hurried in. "Oh, Mr Smith, Mr Smith," she addressed Tammie, "I'm left yon new key on da table and da door is biding shut." We all laughed, but Tammie assured her she would get back in. Tammie and I took a ladder (I later learned an easier way to deal with a jibb lock), and went to the house. We set the ladder up to the window and Tammie went up and opened it. He then came down and said, "Up and in du goes." I climbed in and over the table and opened the door, letting in Tammie and the old lady. "Now," said Tammie, "do you have a piece of string?" When she produced a bit of string, Tammie threaded the key on it and told her to wear it round her neck like a pendant – all day. "Thank you," she said. "You are most kind." She was very appreciative and gave us both a sweetie.

MORE LOCKS

One afternoon a friend set out to go shopping when she noticed her neighbour's curtains was still tightly shut. She thought this was strange so went in the gate and knocked on the door. There was no reply. She tried the door and found it to be keyed. Her neighbour was infirm and could not move around easily, so full of apprehension she went to the bedroom window and knocked. Her knock was answered with the neighbour's voice saying she had slipped on the floor and could not get up. My friend wondered what to do. Should she call the police, or maybe the doctor or the nurse? "No," she thought, "I'd better not, there will only be a fuss and the neighbour will be angry. I'll call Willie."

I happened to be in the workshop so answered the call immediately. I knew the door had a rim lock, so taking a selection of keys plus the little tool I set off for the house, confident that it would be no bother to get it open. The key was in the lock on the inside of the door and I got it pushed out of the way easily. I then tried all the keys I had brought with me and also the little tool. It was no use, however; the door remained tightly locked. "Oh, the poor woman." said my friend, who was standing watching. My only option now was to burst the lock.

A short distance away a man was working on the roof of his house. He was a south man and new to the district. I walked over and told him what was going on and he readily agreed to come and lend a hand. We picked two short battens from the pile of wood in his garden and went back. I got him to hold one of the battens along the door and at the same time turn the door handle. I then hit his batten with the other one and the door flew open.

My friend went into the bedroom, but as her neighbour was quite a hefty woman she found it impossible to get her on the bed by herself, and we were called to assist. As we lifted her off the floor she said to me, "You have burst my lock and I just got it new on last week. You will have to get it properly fixed as it cost me an awful lot of money." We got her sitting on the bed and my friend went to the kitchen to make her tea. I looked at the lock and saw that it had more levers than the keys I had brought or the tool could cope with. It was undamaged and I soon had it replaced and working just like new. As we walked along the road carrying the short battens my sooth helper said, "Now that's what I would call real gratitude."

One night we were sitting having tea when we heard the ding-dong of the doorbell. I opened the door and there stood a woman who said, "I feel such a fool Mr Smith, I've locked myself out. I was going visiting a friend and pulled the door shut before I realised the key was still inside. Do you think you could possibly open the door for me?" Before I could answer she continued, "Now, I'll just go and do my visiting, so whenever you are ready." I said I would finish my tea and then open her door.

Half an hour or so later William, who was a schoolboy at the time, and I set off. We went first to the workshop to collect some tools which would, hopefully, facilitate invisible breaking and entering. Arriving at the house, I looked at the door and got a nasty surprise. The lock was modern and a good bit more advanced than the run of the mill jibb lock. To get this door open was going to be a messy job. I scratched my head, swore under my breath, then said to William, "Lets have a walk around the house." As we walked I looked at the windows – they were not the type of windows you find in most houses today. Soon I found what I was looking for. After two seconds work with a couple of tools the window was open. "OK William," I said. "In you go, shut and fasten the window behind you, then open the door." He clambered in, and, in a moment the door was open and we left for home with me feeling very pleased.

Next day the woman came in the workshop and asked, "What am I due you for opening my door?" "Nothing at all," I said, "it was just seconds' work." "Well, thank you very much indeed, I am most grateful, but how did you do it? There is not a scratch anywhere." I smiled and said, "Ah well, trade secrets, you know. Just accept that your door was open when you got home and there was no damage done. If I were to tell you how, you might not like it." She smiled and said, "If you say so. Once again, thank you."

ME POOR PEERIE BUDGIE

Back in the fifties and sixties not many people had fridges or freezers, so they just took in what food they could use. At the time of year when Vementry lamb was on the go, we – as did every other household – had lamb for breakfast, lamb for dinner, lamb for tea and sometimes lamb for supper as well. I liked Vementry lamb, so for me this was not a problem.

One day we were having casseroled lamb cutlets for dinner, to be followed by another favourite, baked apple pudding. I had just started on the cutlets when, ding dong, went the door bell. When I opened the door, it was to see an elderly lady leaning along the wall. "Oh, me poor peerie budgie. Oh, me poor poor peerie budgie," she said. "What?" I replied, thinking she had flipped her lid. She carried on, "Oh, me poor poor peerie budgie, he's no had his dinner." I thought that made two of us, but decided that maybe I should try and humour her, so I said, "Your budgie has no had his dinner?" She straightened up off the wall and said, "No, no, dat he has not. I'm locked mysel oot, me key is lying on da dresser." That explained everything. I knew her house, and knew that the lock was a jibb lock. "Come," she said. "Come right away!" I thought of the Vementry cutlets growing cold on my plate and told her I would come as soon as I could. "Well you'll have to hurry; me peerie budgie always has his dinner at one o'clock."

When I had finished my cutlets, I thought it might be better to get the budgie seeded before I had my baked apple pudding. I went to the workshop and collected my breaking and entering tools, and some screws and nails just in case. The old lady met me at her gate and led me, not to the door, but to the sitting room window. I was a bit puzzled by this until she pointed to one of the large panes of glass and said, "In here." I then saw that the putty had been cut along one side, along the bottom, and along part of the top. "Who did this?" I asked. "Oh it was Jamie. It was about half past ten in the morning when I got locked out, so I went and fetched Jamie. He could not get the door open, so he started to the glass." I looked at her and said, "Where is he now?" "Oh he had to go for his dinner at one o' clock." I began to feel a bit annoyed, but I thought of my baked apple pudding to come and, staying calm, turned and headed for the door.

I worked away assiduously at the jibb lock, but the lock worked back and refused to open. The continual lamentations at my back about the budgie's dinner started to get to me. I might well have said nasty things about the budgie, Jamie and things in general, when a quiet voice at my shoulder said, "Anything I could do to help?" It was Archie Nicolson and his calm voice and presence defused the situation.

"Yes Archie," I said. "I could use a little help. I should have been able to open this door but I canna, so I'll have to force it open. I would need two short battens." Archie replied, "I have some new fencing posts at the back of my house. Would they do?" "Just the job," I said. So we went to Archie's and came back with two posts. He held one post along the door and turned the handle, and I hit his post with mine. The door flew open and the woman rushed in wailing, "Oh me poor peerie budgie, is du all right my dear? Du sall get dee dinner noo."

The boss head had come off the door post and as I picked it up off the floor Archie asked, "Any damage?" Happily, there was none. All that was needed was a couple of longer screws from the van. I put the new screws in and as Archie and I were going down the path the woman came out and said, "What about the putty on the window? You'll have to fix that." "Send for Jamie," I replied. "He should be finished his dinner by now." We put Archie's posts back to his yard, looked at each other and laughed. I said, "Well, Archie, hungry budgies need dir denner just the same as we do. Dy help is much appreciated, and I suppose all I can say is tanks a lot." He looked at me and said, "My boy, I'm ower blyde tae help, but wha's going tae tank dee? Eh? Eh?"

THE HAND OF GOD?

W e are all familiar, through books and television, with tales of strange happenings that seem to defy rational explanation, and which are difficult to dismiss as simply being due to coincidence. Many years ago I had an experience of this sort, which to this day I am at a loss to explain.

In the mid-sixties an elderly lady, a retired teacher, moved into the village of Scalloway, to a house not far from where I stayed. I worked as a joiner and painter/decorator, so one day she asked me if I would come and paint her windows and doors. She liked to talk and, as I worked, she would often come and chat with me.

Some time later, I got into the habit of visiting her every Friday evening for a half hour or so. We would sit and talk and when I left I would take her refuse bag and set it ready for the Saturday morning collection. I enjoyed my chats with her, as she was a very interesting person and could talk on many subjects. She did not appear to have many friends so I am sure that she enjoyed my Friday evening visits and our conversations, regardless of the fact that I carried out her refuse bag. I visited her every Friday evening for a long time; the only other time I went along was if she asked me to do something specific.

Now to the event which I thought about for a long time afterwards. Many of us have taken the car out, arrived at our destination, then suddenly realised that we had little recollection of the journey; in other words we had driven most of the way on automatic pilot! Well, one summer evening I was walking along the street when I suddenly found myself opening the old lady's gate and walking along the path towards her back door. As it was not a Friday, I started to feel very uncomfortable. However, I was in full view of both her's and the neighbours' windows so I carried on.

The old lady always kept her door keyed except on a Friday evening when she knew I would call. I decided I would quietly try the door, which I confidently expected to be keyed, then make a quick exit down the path. Much to my surprise the door opened at my touch. I went in and opened the kitchen door. The old lady was sitting by the fire and one glance told me she was a very ill woman. I said, "Hello," and she replied, "Am I glad to see you. I've been sitting here praying that you would call and my prayer has been answered." She was seriously ill and had to be rushed to hospital for an emergency operation.

What directed me to the old lady's door that night? She prayed to God for me to call. Did God guide my footsteps to her door? I don't know, but that night, without my visit, she would surely have died.

A TALE FROM WATLEE

In my younger days I was a keen angler. In the mid-fifties and early sixties I did a lot of loch fishing in Unst. The loch I fished most was the Loch of Watlee, which lies in a valley with the hill of Valla Field on one side and the hill of Colvadale on the other. In those days my transport was a Lambretta scooter, registration PS2821, and it could take me right to the side of the loch. The south end of Watlee could be accessed from the main Uyeasound to Baltasound road, by what used to be just a peat track. People at that time were still working peats on the west side of Watlee and they boated the peats across the loch to near the road.

When I set out for Watlee I would strap my rod and bag to the carrier of the scooter. I then rolled the scooter off the stand, turned on the petrol, pulled out the choke and started the engine. After it had run for a moment I would push in the choke and set off. Arriving at the loch side, I would take the rod out of it's cover, assemble it, fit on the reel and line, tie on a spinner or bubble float and hook and start fishing. The rod then had to be disassembled when it was time to go home.

About two thirds along the east side of the loch there is a promontory. I fished both sides of the loch, but my favourite spots were the east side and beyond the promontory. Almost every time I fished in

At Watlee Loch. © *Vera Smith*

A good night's catch. © *Vera Smith*

Watlee I caught trout, sometimes maybe only one. My best catch was seven in one night.

I was fascinated by Watlee for some unknown reason. It seemed that I was always being called back. On a fine sunny day it was a lovely place, peaceful and tranquil. But when the weather was misty, dull and overcast I seemed to sense a change of mood – dark, brooding and sinister. I gave very little thought to this change of aspect until, that is, a distinctly unpleasant experience brought it to my full attention.

It was on a still, overcast evening in August that I arrived at the Loch of Watlee. Apart from the bleating of the sheep on the hills, the only sounds to be heard were the clicks from my fishing reel as I swapped out and reeled in the spinner. I fished along the east side of the loch towards and past the promontory but, contrary to my expectations, the loch appeared to be completely dormant, not even a single fish stirred. Bemused, I carried on northwards and soon realised that I had walked much further than I had meant to. I turned about and headed back to the south, fishing as I went.

By the time I was approaching the scooter it was quite dusky. On all my previous visits to the loch I had left within the hours of daylight. When about ten yards or so from the scooter I suddenly became aware that I was not alone. It was a strange creepy feeling. I stopped and looked all around, but could see nothing. It was with unease that I moved on. I was then struck by an overpowering feeling that something unseen and malevolent was coming towards me from the north, and I could feel its presence getting nearer and stronger.

Overcome now by fear, I started to run. I jumped astride the scooter, rolled off the stand, turned on the petrol, pulled out the choke and kicked the start pedal. The engine fired first kick, I engaged gear and accelerated flat out for the main road without looking back, the hairs on my neck standing on end. The scooter rattled and jarred as it was driven at top speed along the rough track. In my terror I feared I would never make the main road. I could feel the evil presence pursuing me, getting closer every second. Suddenly I had crossed onto the main road and the presence, feeling, whatever it was, had completely vanished.

I braked and came to a stop. The choke was still out and my rod lay along the handlebars. I looked all around and waited, hopeful that at last I was indeed alone. As I sensed nothing more, I stopped the engine and rolled the scooter onto her stand. There was not a breath of wind, not a sound, except for the nick nick of the scooter engine cooling.

I dismantled my fishing tackle and tied the rod in its case on the carrier of the scooter. I then pushed in the choke, started the engine again and headed for Uyeasound. It was quite dark when I arrived back at Batavia. I was by then wondering if my strange and fearful experience had indeed really happened – but I knew it had.

Next day I went back to Watlee and walked north past the promontory. Everything was peaceful and calm, but I had a slight feeling of unease. I fished the Loch of Watlee many times after that, but always made a point of leaving with daylight in the sky.

Today, many years on, I am convinced there was intense evil afoot that night. If my scooter had failed to start, who knows, I might not have made it to the main road. In fact I'm sure of it. The memory of these few terror filled moments I know will stay with me always. However, when I told the folks at Batavia, no one seemed at all surprised. Maybe others also have a tale of Watlee.

THE LIGHTER SIDE OF UNDERTAKING

Funeral undertaking and funerals, are for the most part very sombre and distressing affairs. But looking back over many years some funerals I have attended have been quite hilarious. I had not been working long when I was put to help Uncle Robbie make a coffin. In those days, and for many years after, coffins were made out of Scots fir and covered with plain black cloth. Fancy ormolu lace and gold painted handles and plates were then added to the sides and lid. The inside was padded, the lining was white embossed cloth with purple trimmings and purple headed tacks. It all had to be done very reverently and particularly. There was no rushing and there could be no mistakes.

About six months into work and at fifteen years of age, I went with my brother Tammie to a kisting. I was not impressed. With three bereavements in the family leaving an impression on my mind, I said undertaking was not going to be part of my life. However like everything else you get used to things. What follows now will be one of the occasions that has made us smile. I am not trying to make fun of death or the dead, its just life.

I suppose the most humorous occasion (although not at the time), was the funeral of an old travelling man. He was to be buried in his home area in Scotland so the funeral had to be on a day when the *St Clair* was sailing. My brother Tammie and Geordie Nicolson went to the kisting. At the door they were met by the eldest son, who was well and truly intoxicated. Tammie and Geordie were great diplomats when dealing with bereaved people, but more so in this instance with the man in charge very, very drunk. After the kisting had taken place the son said, "I'm very sorry gentlemen, I cannot offer you a refreshment as it was the old man's wish, there was to be no drink." As both men had refrained from strong drink all their lives there was no problem, and they assured him that they quite understood

It was winter time and the day of the funeral was dull and overcast, but dry. We were to meet at the house about twenty to two. The family and friends had all gathered, women folk in the kitchen and the men in the front lobby where Tammie, Geordie and I met them. The old man's brother, a nephew, a grandson and his two sons were all very drunk. The oldest son, drunk as he was, very efficiently greeted everyone, shook their hand and bade them welcome, and said he was pleased they could come.

Chairs had been set in line in the living room and already neighbour men and some from outside Scalloway were seating themselves. Soon the minister arrived, Rev Isaac Ralph, who was also greeted by the son. Two o'clock came and Tammie nodded to the minister who then started the service. As he read from the Bible the second son made oobin sounds but was quietened by the elbow of the oldest son. When Rev Ralph finished the Bible readings he said, "Let us join together in prayer." Heads were bowed, in the kitchen, living room and in the front lobby. As he progressed into the prayer, I do not recall his exact words but the old man's brother took exception and said, "Hey, hey, that's nae right."

The oldest son who was standing as erect as a soldier on parade suddenly sprang to life said to the minister, "Hold on a minute now," grabbed his uncle by the collar of his jacket, twisted an arm behind his back and ran him through the living room full of bowed headed men, through the kitchen with weeping women and literally, threw him out the back door onto the green. The son then shut and keyed the back door, shut the kitchen door, shut the living room door, then said to the minister, "Right, you can carry on now." While all this was going on, no one in the front lobby had moved. I sneaked a look round and corners of mouths were twitching.

The Rev had just restarted his prayer when we heard the crash of the back door glass coming in. The prayer and service were finished so we went to the bedroom to take out the coffin. Tammie was going to carry at the head and Geordie at the foot. I was to take the trestles. They had just lifted the coffin when the son, who had now got his coat on, came charging through the lobby, "Hold on a minute now, put it down, put it down." They reset the coffin back on the trestles. We looked at one another and were all thinking, what now.

The son pushed Tammie to the side and said, "I'll carry at the head, its my old man you know, its the old man." The son and Geordie lifted, Tammie signalled to me to walk by Geordie, while he walked by the son. Considering the state of drink the son was in you could not fault him for the very stately way he carried his father's coffin. The hearse in those days was a minibus, which we all reached without mishap. It was the only funeral I was ever at where the minister left the house with a huge grin on his face.

In those days men walked behind the hearse, up the road to the school, then got in cars or buses. Of the family men, the oldest son was the only one to walk behind the hearse, in fact he was probably the only one who could walk. It was dusky by the time we got to the steamer's store in Lerwick. The coffin had to be put in a case for shipment to Aberdeen. As we did not have such a case we borrowed one from Duncan and Bolt. After closing the case the dockers took over and the last we saw of the old travelling man was being lowered by crane into the hold of the *St Clair* for his onward travels to his final resting place. The son came and shook hands with us all and so we made our way home to Scalloway.

MORE ON THE LIGHTER SIDE

One morning I was having my ten o'clock's when the phone rang. Chewing on a piece of Black's water biscuit I answered, "Hello." A voice said, "Is yon dee Willie?" and when I agreed it was, continued, "Dis is Jim, boy I'm not seen dee in a while, foo is du?" Jim, I knew, but not awful well. We spoke about this and that, the weather etc. and I was beginning to wonder if it was just a social call when he said, "This morning we noticed there was no reek fae auld grandfather's lum, so I went along and he had just slept away, can du come along now?" I agreed to meet Jim at grandfather's in an hour.

Grandfather stayed on a croft and as I drove up the road I noticed the crofthouse was very neglected looking, unpainted windows and door and lots of bruk all around. Jim was there and as we went into the house my joiner's nose, used to the smell of red pine and fine woods, detected the smell of rotting timber. The rooms were not large but quite tidy and clean.

As we went up the stair, which was narrow, steep and had a vicious turn at the top, with a landing flanked by a coom ceiling, Jim wondered if we would ever get a coffin up there. After, as you might say, casting a professional eye over the stair, I agreed it could be done but just. "What about getting it down again?" asked Jim. "You know the old saying," I said, "What goes up must come down. If the coffin can go up the stair it will go down, but with a little more effort." When we went into the bedroom I asked if the doctor had been. "Oh, yes," said Jim, "came right away." "So there is no problem about the certificate then." "Well, he said he would have to phone the police and they would send a man out." "So he's been and everything is OK." "Na, na, no yet, he'll be shortly, but that's no needing to hinder dee." I said we would touch nothing until the policeman had been.

We went down stair and after about thirty minutes or so heard a car coming up the road. It was a police car and in it was a sergeant. He introduced himself and shook hands. The Sergeant was a hefty guy and as the three of us climbed up the stair it creaked ominously. After a look at old grandfather and all around the room, and some questions to Jim, the sergeant said he was satisfied and would phone the doctor to issue a certificate. He also said I could go ahead and do what I had to do but would it not be difficult getting the coffin down stair? Maybe he'd better stay and give me a hand. I said "Well, I have to go to Scalloway and prepare the coffin. Thanks for your offer but I won't have the coffin ready until after tea time." He says "I have to see someone in this area at six tonight so I will look as I go past, if your van is here I'll be quite willing to help." With that he left. I did what was necessary, took measurements and left for Scalloway.

I phoned Jim at teatime and told him I should be at the house about quarter to seven. I was and we got the coffin up stair with a bit of effort. Jim thought it was going to be a different story with the old man in it, and hoped the sergeant would turn up. We got the lid off the coffin, laid out the side sheets, lifted old grandfather in, then set the coffin up on two trestles. Jim, I might add, was a reluctant helper, some folk are like that.

In my early days I was told it was the living to watch out for, not the dead. However he did help. After I had put the side sheets back, straightened and smoothed and all that, I went to the foot of the coffin and looked. Old grandfather's head was ever so slightly looking towards the right. Moving to the head of the coffin I eased the side sheets, took his head in both hands and twisted so he was now looking straight ahead. I put the side sheets back and as we looked the head turned, so once more he was looking towards the right. Taking his head in both hands again I twisted, and once again the head turned. At this I looked at Jim and Jim looked at me and said, "He was a stiff necked old bugger all his life, does du think he is going to alter for dee now even though he's dead." I lifted the side sheets once more and put a little pad under his right shoulder. This straightened the head and with a sigh of relief I put the side sheets back in place for the last time. We had just got the lid on the coffin when we heard a car, it was the police sergeant.

The sergeant came in and up stair. "Just in time," said Jim. "We're all ready to move down stair." With the stair being almost vertical the coffin would have to be nearly standing on end to get it down. I suggested that I would take the foot and move down resting the coffin one step at a time. Jim and the sergeant were to hold and take the weight. Slowly we made our way down, Jim and the sergeant close together at the head. The room that the coffin was to rest in was the ben room. To get to the ben room I would have to take the foot of the coffin into the kitchen still almost vertical. Every step the stair creaked.

Having reached the floor level the sergeant lowered and I lifted, taking a step backwards as I did so. As my weight, plus the weight of the coffin came on my right foot there was a cracking noise and I felt my foot starting to go through the floor. I was much more agile than I am today. I gave a little hop and a skip and got on solid wood. It is not something I would have admitted at the time, but I was very apprehensive and tensed up about this whole operation. Jim and I were average sized men but the sergeant was that little bit heavier, so it meant three men and grandfather in the stair at one time. After the hop and skip and finding my feet on solid wood, tension was released and I said a lot of inexcusable and unprintable words. Jim had got the trestles from the bedroom so we set the coffin in the ben room. There it would stay until the funeral day.

We stood outside for a while and spoke, then the sergeant laughed, "I don't think I'll ever forget the sound of the floor cracking, the little dance and the swear words." As it could have been quite serious I have not forgot it either.

MINA'S

I n this day and age card playing is like many other things, a part of life. In my young days however, playing card games was frowned on by many people. It was the bad man's cards or Da Deil's Books. Some folk played and others, never. Card playing was not part of our household and I never played cards until I was about fifteen years old.

Let me tell you about Peerie Mina's shop. Situated on the main street in Scalloway, where the lounge of the hotel now stands, the shop sold apples, oranges, greeting cards, toys and lots and lots of fancy goods.

The highlight of any youngster's day, if they had a penny or two, was Mina's ice cream. The blocks of ice came from the ice factory in Lerwick. In the back shop was an ice grinder and I can remember on occasions being allowed to turn the handle. When the war really started to bite we used to queue for a cone or a slider, if we had money that day. Mina was only allowed to make a small quantity and it was ready by half past ten in the morning. Most days it was all finished by twenty

Scalloway Hotel and Mina's Shop. © *C.J.W.*

to eleven. Mina was a very friendly person, and to the young, very kindly indeed.

When I reached the grand old age of fifteen, I, like many others thought and felt grown up. So I started to join the group of men who always met in Mina's after tea. The shop was open until at least ten. Some men stood in the shop all evening, others just for a while, or perhaps to trade a few stories and get someone excited.

Across the lifting part of the counter a card game was always in progress. Rummy was the name of the game and I always tried to get a bit closer to watch. At first I was just ignored by the older men, but I got to be accepted and greeted as time went by. I listened to all the yarns and

Mina Nicolson and Jonnie Philips.   © C.J.W.

stories that were told, some were directed at my young ears but I gradually learned to sift the corn from the chaff.

One man told of working at the farm of Utnabrake. The cats, he said, were a pest, leaving messes here and there. One day he took an egg and went to the bin where the hens' meal was kept. He made a small hollow in the meal and broke the egg into it, then covered it over. When the boss came to get meal for the hens he thought he was in a cat's mess. Cats were not in favour for a while.

One night, a man told a story which at the time seemed just like a yarn, but I learned later it was true. It was during the first war, he said, he had got fed up with the army so decided to head north and try to get home to Shetland. He worked at various jobs on his way through the country and in Aberdeenshire got a job on a farm. After a few weeks,

Mina's Shop. © *C.J.W.*

when he had some money, he made his only purchase, a new pair of boots. One day he thumbed a lift into Aberdeen. There he went to the docks where he saw a trawler lying at a jetty. He asked one of the crew where they were going and the man said Shetland. Thinking this really meant Shetland he asked if they needed any crew. As they did, he signed on. On the trawler heading north he found out that was a big mistake. They'd actually meant the Shetland fishing grounds. As another trawler came alongside so the skippers could talk (wireless on boats was just something of the future), he calmly stepped from one trawler to the other. This, he said, was another mistake, because he was now heading back to Aberdeen and his new boots, which had been laid off for an old pair of wellies, were now heading for the fishing grounds. He said he hid for a while suffering extreme vexation on account of his fine boots. So it was back to Aberdeen and no pay.

Jimmy Wishart told me when he was a young lad, one night he was sent to Mina's after tea to get some Black Twist for Uncle Henry. As usual it was full of men. Some were telling stories and others were having a discussion. The discussion he heard was, if you had to lose one of your senses, which would you be prepared to lose and why. Jimmy listened to all they said, but what stuck in his mind most was when it came to John Ross' turn, he said he would lose his hearing. When asked why, John replied that he would not then have to listen to the utter rubbish always talked in the shop.

Back to the card players. I watched the rummy game many nights and soon knew what it was all about. One night, that was the big night, when I came in the shop there were only two men there, Charlie Paton and James Willum Duncan. When I came into the light Mina said, "Oh here's Willie, I'm sure he can play, come dee wis in ahint da coonter wi me." Mina, not being very tall, always stood on a stool to play. My goodness, I felt at least eight feet tall and twenty-five years old, being invited to play. I don't remember who won or much about the game, but that was my first time playing cards. After that I was always at Mina's early every night so I would get a chance to play. After a while they started to play gin rummy, then sometimes whist.

Still the stories were told. Some of the men who were regular callers and story tellers were Peter Twatt, Willie Burnet, Angus Moore, John W. Slater, Peter Laurenson, Peerie John, Robbie Hardy and there were many others. Sometimes Teenie and Jessie would come in and wind some of the older ones up, until insults were flying all around the shop. Voices would be raised and you laughed till your sides were sore. Next day it would all be as normal, as if nothing had been said, and no one took any offence.

Later in life I went to whist drives in the hall and the recreation club but they never ever had the atmosphere of playing rummy in Mina's. Sadly, Peerie Mina's shop is no more and I look back with nostalgia to those days, playing Da Deils Books across Mina's counter, with stories, arguments and light hearted banter in the background.

A SWEEPING TALE

I n 1945, with the war just finished, I began my working career as an apprentice joiner with a Scalloway building firm. We did a lot of school maintenance work and travelled to schools all over the Mainland, from West Burrafirth to Bridge End, Brae to Cunningsburgh. It was an interesting time for a young lad starting work.

I already knew most of my fellow workmates, if not very well. However, I soon got to know them much better. One of the men I enjoyed working with was known as Peerie Jeck. He was called Peerie Jeck, not because he was peerie, but because he had been given the same name as his father. Jeck was something of a practical joker. He got up to all sorts of tricks and you needed to keep your wits about you when you were in his company. We always had lots of laughs when working together, as Jeck was full of amusing stories. This is a story he told me many years ago.

It had been a busy summer, with a lot of work to be done. One of the small rural schools had not been visited during the holidays, so on

Peerie Jeck.   © *Willie Smith*

a Saturday morning late in August, Jeck and three other men set out to do the overdue maintenance work. One of the jobs to be done was to sweep the chimney. This was done using the simplest of equipment. There were no fancy rods and chimney brush; just a length of rope, an iron ball and a large bunch of heather. The heather was gathered from the roadside on the outward journey.

This school, like many others in Shetland at that time, had only one teacher, who was a married lady. Her husband stayed at home, doing most of the housework and cooking the meals. He was a trifle absent minded.

When Jeck and his workmates arrived there was no one

Lum sweeping with heather and ball.
© C.J.W.

to be seen. It was Saturday, after all, and the teacher and her husband were having a long lie. A stiff breeze was blowing and as it seemed that the wind was getting stronger, Jeck decided to sweep the lum first. As the other men went off to do various jobs, he put up the ladders and then went into the schooroom and made the fireplace ready. Climbing up the ladders, he soon reached the chimney and began lowering the ball and heather down.

He was partly finished when he saw the teacher's husband standing on the lawn below. "Hello," he greeted Jeck. "Do you think you could sweep our kitchen chimney too?" "Yes, certainly," Jeck replied. "Get everything ready and then give me a shout." The teacher's husband looked pleased. "I'll do that. Thank you very much." Before long, he was back out on the lawn. Waving an arm aloft, he shouted, "It's all ready now."

Jeck was nimble and very sure footed. He was unhindered by the breeze as he stepped along the ridge of the roof to the kitchen lum. Kneeling on the chimney stack, he lowered the ball and heather down, hauled it back up, then lowered it again. After he had done this enough times to give the chimney a good clean, he gathered up his equipment, came down off the roof and took down the ladders. He then lit a cigarette and stood watching some birds in a nearby field for a few minutes, before going into the school to remove the soot and clean the fireplace.

Upon entering the school, Jeck's attention was drawn to a gurgling sound. He walked through the corridor towards the strange sound and discovered one of his workmates doubled up, helpless with laughter. All the man could manage to do was raise his arm and point out of the side window. A good breeze was blowing through the passageway formed by the schoolhouse gable and some adjacent sheds. Standing at the entrance to this passageway seemed to be a gentleman of African extraction, his mouth wide open, gasping like a fish out of water. Jeck stared in amazement as he realised that this black man was in fact the teacher's husband.

Almost overcome with mirth, Jeck ran to the schoolhouse and dashed into the kitchen. The sight that met his eyes quickly dispelled all thoughts of laughter. Absolutely everything was covered in a thick layer of soot. The clock on the mantle, the dishes on the dresser, the chairs, the once white table cloth – everything had a good, thick covering of soot. And the footprints on the floor revealed a black impression of the pattern on the waxcloth.

As Jeck surveyed the mess, the husband came in and explained what had happened. The kitchen fire was a Bonnybridge Dover Range. It had a metal backplate, with a sliding door for easing the draught, and was a forerunner of the more advanced Rayburn stoves with sootboxes and tiled surrounds. The old man had not noticed, he said, that the draught hole was open, so when the iron ball and heather came down the lum, the soot poured out of the hole and into the room. He had grappled with the sliding door in a desperate attempt to close it, but had been covered in soot and forced to beat a retreat. To make matters worse, he had thought he had better tell his wife, who was still in bed and unaware of the drama being enacted out downstairs. He had gone to tell her, forgetting to shut the door below, with the result that the hallway and stair were now also black with soot.

Jeck said to him, "I think you should go and wash your face." As he went off to do this, Jeck fetched a shovel and bucket to clean up with. The Bonnybridge was piled high with soot. As he dug into it the shovel hit something solid – it was the kettle, completely 'moored up'.

It was a very angry school teacher who appeared downstairs that morning. What should have been a leisurely day off was now going to be far worse than her week's work. Jeck started to apologise, but she would have none of it. "It's not your fault," she said. "It's that old fool over there," as she pointed to her cowering husband. "And get that dirty jumper off!" The old fellow then grasped his jumper at the bottom and hauled it over his head, leaving his newly washed face almost as black as before. Jeck did not know whether to laugh or to cry, but he helped the teacher and her husband clean up the worst of the mess before going back to finish his own work. There was much laughter when he went to the schoolroom and told the other men what had taken place that morning.

I heard the above story told many times, but writing it down can never convey the impact it had when told by 'Peerie Jeck'.

FROM SANDNESS TO HASLEY KNOB
(and back)

One night in early March 2000, I got a phone call from my old friend in Melby, Bertie Jamieson. I call him my old friend because he is six months older than I am (sorry Bertie). "Boy," he said, "what about wis going to the National Standard Car Rally?" "Hits in Hasley Knob, Warwickshire."

Bertie has a 1934 Standard Ten classic car with which we have toured in Norway and Faroe previously. We never had any problems, the old car ran like a beauty. However, there was one time we went up a mountain in Norway, which was so steep the petrol could not reach the engine from the gravity fed tank at the back of the car. We had to be rescued by Andrew Morrison, but we don't talk about that. "Yes, we'll go," I said, "but Haseley Knob, where tae yon place is that?" "Way down in England, past Birmingham and Coventry and places like that, a piece of cake to folk like wis," said Bertie. I believed him implicitly.

On Tuesday, 27th June, 2000 at 5pm, with me in the passenger seat and Bertie at the wheel, the 1934 Standard Ten boarded the *St Clair* for Aberdeen. After we got the car settled for the night we went to look for our two berth cabin. I said, "I suppose the youngest one will have to get in the top bunk." Bertie's reply was, "Du can please dysel, but I most certainly will be getting in the lower one!" We had something to eat, a peerie dram, a yarn with Annie and Billy Nicolson, and it was a fine smooth run to Aberdeen.

We left the *St Clair* at 8am and headed through Torry and Nigg and joined the main road at Charlestown to the south, looking forward to whatever adventures might come our way. The weather was fine and sunny until we reached Brechin, then it rained for a while. The old Standard was running like a beauty and clocking along at a steady 50 mph. We stopped at Glamis for a wee while (if you get my meaning!), and after we passed by Perth and Stirling we stopped and had a cup of tea.

I then took the wheel and we carried on along the A74. Some time later we stopped at a roadside café for a meal and to relax a little. Bertie then took the wheel and we went by Gretna. We didn't see anyone on the green or any wedding parties. We bypassed Carlisle and on to the M6. When we saw a big sign saying Southwaite Service Station we headed in that road and on to a Travelodge. I should say that on the M6 driving was no bother, even for two old fellows like us. Cars would toot their horns, flash their lights and generally acknowledge a real car. Huge artic trucks would sail past us and flash their indicators and lights. They looked just like Christmas trees.

I went in to the Lodge to see if they had a room for two Shelties and had to wait while two Americans got booked in. The lady behind the desk had an extremely white complexion. I was not listening to their conversation but I was there and I could not help but hear it. I suppose I could have sung or hummed, then I would not have heard, but who cares. The gist of it was that the American lady could not bear much sunlight, though what this had to do with staying the night in a Lodge I do not know. The lady behind the desk then said she could not go out in sunlight at all or her face blistered, and she had to be very careful even in daylight. I thought how lucky I was, to be able to sit out in the sunshine. What am I talking about? Sunshine in Shetland, ah well, one can but dream.

After a while they got themselves sorted out and it was my turn. A twin room, no bother at all. I asked if we could get one on the ground floor as my friend would not be too happy with stairs. That also was no problem, and was I a member of the AA? I didn't see what having a wee dram had to do with booking a room, until she said they gave a discount to members of the Automobile Association! So we got a room for the night and a discount on Bertie's AA card. No meal that night, just tea and biscuits and some TV.

On Thursday 29th at 9.45am we joined the M6 again and were soon bowling along at a steady 50mph towards Penrith, then diverting towards Keswick. The road to Keswick is typical rural England, fields, trees, flowers and very nice countryside. We found a coffee shop in Keswick and relaxed for a while, then went looking for a car museum Bertie had heard about. It was a bit of a disappointment as it contained cars of film stars, such as Batman, Laurel and Hardy, 007, Mr Bean and lots of others; no classic cars! I had a video camera and a 35mm camera hanging on my arm, but two men were on watch to see that a 'no photos' ban was adhered too. We thought our money would have been better left in our pockets, but that's life.

So we left Keswick and took the A591 towards Windermere. Past Lake Thirlmere and on to Grasmere. Then we drove by Lake Windermere, on the scenic trail, the road turning and twisting, just like the road to Sandness, but trees, trees everywhere, with just a glimpse of water now and then. Oh, did I mention the rain? It was bucketing down, just like home. Never mind, lovely countryside but best on foot, not in a classic car on the way to a rally.

So it was on to junction 36 and once more we were on the M6. After a while we felt a bit hungry so when we saw a Little Chef at Forton, Bertie headed the dear little old car in that direction for a late lunch. It was food by the mile, but we were hungry. Hunger abated, I took the wheel and once more we bowled along at a steady 50mph. When junction 19 near Knutsford was approaching, by a unanimous decision, that dear little old car headed for the nearest toilet. After that comfort stop, Bertie once more took the wheel and drove on to Stafford services near junction 14. There we found a very nice Lodge, just like a hotel.

We got in about 6pm and settled for the night. About half past eight some idiot in the room upstair decided to do their keep fit routine. They leapt up and down, bump and dad, with a regularity just like clockwork. It went on and on, the ceiling birred and shook and still they leapt up and down, like a yo-yo. Bertie said,"Hand me da broom an a'll dad on da roof." Fortunately there was no broom. At this point I refuse to write the things two aged, much respected, senior citizen Shelties said about the keep fit twits, parentage, mentality and general outlook on life.

Friday morning dawned fine but very misty. We left Stafford at 10am with Bertie at the wheel. After a time it started to rain, it was really heavy and not good driving weather on the M6. When we saw a sign which read Corley Services, we suddenly remembered we needed food. I won't go into detail about what Bertie ate, but I had bacon, egg, tomato and chips, followed by a very tasty fruit cocktail. I don't really mean a cocktail it was just a plate with a lot of fruit on it! A nice cup of tea and Bertie and I were ready for the road again.

We left Corley and took the M6 until we came to the A446 and then the A4177 which took us to Hasley Knob. We were to stay at a guest house called the Croft House, where we arrived at 12.55pm. From Sandness, the little old car had already travelled 504 miles. Didn't she do well? It was very quiet at the Croft House and once more we had a

Two Standards at the Croft House.   © *W.S.*

ground floor room. After checking in we had a very peaceful afternoon, but at half past five the hunt was on for food. We set off along the Haseley road and found The Falcon, which served bar meals. I had lamb flank, new tatties and vegetables, and Bertie had roast duck and chips. It was all very tasty and went down a real treat. When we got back to the Croft House three more Standards had arrived; a 1933 Standard 16, colour green, VN4932; a 1953 Standard Pennant, grey above and black below, 847BAF; a Standard 10, light grey, over 300,000 miles, SHP848. This car was painted with Dulux paint and the job done with a paint roller!

On Saturday, 1st July, we left the Croft House at 9.20am for Hatton, to assemble for a run to Coventry Standard Recreation Club. About twenty or so cars took part. Everyone got a map showing how to get there. As I was the one with the map with multifarious streets, crossroads and criss cross crossroads, I said to Bertie he had better not lose sight of the Standard ahead of us. He was as good as my word and the fact that we went through five red lights to do it, ah well, who was counting! Of course, we haven't told anyone that.

After a brief stop at the club we went on to the Midland Air Museum where, as a special concession to the Standard Club, we were allowed to take the cars in among the planes for photos. It was not a fine day, no wind but drizzling wet. We got back to Hatton about 2.30pm and went to Hatton Country World for a late lunch. Now it rained, really heavy and just as suddenly it stopped and the sun came

Bertie with Standard at Midland Air Museum. © *W.S.*

out, shirt sleeve weather and hot. By this time there were about 85 Standard cars on the showfield. People stopped to speak. "Shetland, oh yes, that's in the Western Isles!" One man said he came from Wales and had thought he might get the prize for the furthest travelled Standard, "But," he said, "you will get that for sure coming from Shetland." As it

Bertie and others with 1933 Standard 16.
© *W.S.*

happens, Bertie and the dear little old car did not get the prize, but did get a special mention. They awarded the prize to a car from Switzerland. Of us two Shelties I was the more annoyed, it was, after all, billed as a National rally, not an International one. Enough said!

On Sunday we had a leisurely breakfast and got to the showfield at 10am. It was a fine day with the sun just offering to shine, warm and sticky. There were a lot more cars. I think the total was 97 altogether. Some of the cars arrived on trailers, one in particular looking like it had just come off the mantelpiece, not a speck of dust anywhere. There was much car talk and lifting of bonnets, car bonnets that is. Bertie and I went and had lunch at The Greedy Pig and very good it was. The show finished at 4.30pm and we set off back to the Croft House. Later we went and had a meal at the Gallery Restaurant then turned in for an early night.

On Monday 3rd. at 10am, we set off for the north, hoping for an uneventful run. We had a brief watering stop at Keele, then at 1.45 stopped at Charnock Richard service station for something to eat. As usual we attracted a bit of attention, at least the Standard Ten did. A large building housed various shops and the usual eatery, which we made for. I noted, for future reference, the toilets just inside the main door of the complex.

At the eatery we had a main course and coffee. At a table to our left sat a man and woman. At a table behind us were two women and three children. It was not a busy time in the dining area. Halfway through coffee Bertie said, "Notice any toilets anywhere?" Was I no a clever boy an able tae tell him! As we were talking, the man and woman got up and left. Bertie went to the toilet. As he did so a man came hurrying into the dining area and went somewhere behind me. He did not go to the counter and he was not carrying any eatables. He was well dressed and ordinary looking, except for his eyes, which, I could not help but notice, were wide and staring.

With the usual childish chatter the three children and two women passed by where I was sitting and went out. I suddenly realised only staring eyes and myself were in the dining area. Where was he and what was he up to? Without turning round I tried to look to the left, no sign of him, then I tried to look to the right, still no sign of him. A bit alarmed, I turned right round.

You know how bairns get a big plate of food set before them, sausage, chips, tomato, a slice of toast, and so on, and just eat some of it. Grown ups of course do this too. Well, to my astonishment there was staring eyes, bent over the folk's table and with a spoon shovelling the left overs into his mouth, as fast as he could, hardly taking time to chew. My first reaction was to grab for my video camera, but fearing a scene I didn't, but continued to watch. He cleaned first one plate, then all the others, calmly collected the plates, knives, forks, put them on a tray and headed for the counter. At this point one of the staff was heading towards the table where the man and woman had been sitting. Staring eyes held out the tray to her. She completely ignored him. He went to the counter and held out the tray to a girl at the cash point, but she too ignored him, so he set the tray on the counter and hurried out. Obviously he was known to them, maybe he was the garbage man! Bertie returned and we left.

As we were getting into the Standard, a car stopped right in front of us and the driver, a smiling man, approached. I said, "Oh dear, oh dear, here is another classic car fanatic." But it was not so. It was a salesman, an Italian, travelling in women's underwear, (not literally of course), from European fashion houses. "Hallo, my good friends. I have many samples which I do not wanta to take home with me so I sell them all to you good men for half price, wot do you say?" We told him ever so gently to get lost, or words to that effect. The smile disappeared and lots of Italian words came off him, which fortunately we did not understand.

With me at the wheel we were on the road again, stopping briefly at Burton in Kendal and on to Tenbay, where Bertie took over and we arrived at Southwaite service station for the night. It was very warm driving, so we had the side windows open and the windscreen as well. It was 202 miles from the Croft House. We had a sumptuous repast at a Little Chef. It was so exciting I can't remember what it was.

On Tuesday morning we had a long wait for breakfast. There were so many hungry people and the Little Chef staff were just run off their feet. We left Southwaite at 10.30am and at junction 44 left the motorway and took the tourist route to Edinburgh. After a very leisurely run through fine countryside we stopped in Hawick for some lunch. At about 4pm we drove into Dalkeith Road, Edinburgh, and a traffic hold up. One and a half hours it took us to get to the Meadows. Bertie was going to his son, Alan and I was going to my daughter, Kristine.

On Friday, 7th July, we left Edinburgh after spending two pleasant days with wir respective bairns and dir folk. Soon we were rolling northwards and heading for our next car rally, the Glamis Extravaganza. Approaching Dalgety Bay, Bertie said there was a Waas man, Willie Moar, staying there and we would go and see him. We turned off at Dalgety Bay and when Bertie looked for his address, it was

Some of the 97 Standard cars.　　　　　　　　　　　　© *W.S.*

not among the papers, but his phone number was. We called him but got no answer. Straight ahead from where we had stopped was a restaurant, so decided to have an early lunch. When we drove into the car park, a lot of faces appeared at a window, and as we went in a woman said, "I love your car," to which Bertie replied, "So do I."

After a very nice lunch we had just reached the car when my mobile phone rang. I answered and a voice asked if I had been calling. It was Willie Moar, so we got his address and had a visit with him and lots of yarns.

Leaving Dalgety Bay we were as usual talking away and soon I said to Bertie that we seemed to be heading for the Forth Road Bridge, and we were. We had no option but to once more cross the bridge, then turn and come back again. We did yak a lot! The problem now was how far did we have to go before we could turn. Where was Andrew Morrison now? Going on a downhill gradient, suddenly we saw a road turning off left and this the little old car turned into.

After a while I said to Bertie, "This road is awful narrow, more so than any road on the wast side of Shetland." Trees everywhere of course, but soon the road straightened and we could see a man standing to his middle in a manhole. The manhole, needless to say was right in the middle of the road. On the other side was a British Telecom van. The Standard stopped about ten feet behind the man. I got out to speak but there was such a racket of noise coming from the dual carriageway that he was unaware of me until I knelt in front of him. I said, "Any idea where we could turn round so we can head north?" "Where are you?" he asked. I pointed behind him, he turned round then started to laugh, "That's a cycle track, just how to hell did you get there?" I said, "Its easy, its just a little car." Still laughing he said if we would give him a minute while he sorted some wires he would let us past and give us directions. There must have been about two or three hundred wires. When he was finished, it was on the phone to check, then on with the manhole lid. He then gave us directions how to get to a U turn and soon the little car was once more heading north.

The pressure eased noticeably and the yaking started up again! It was a straight run then to Forfar and on to check in with Mr and Mrs Powell at their house set in farm country. Kristine had a folding pram she wanted to send to Scalloway so she wondered if we could take it in the car. With two suitcases, welly boots and lots of purchases there was not much room, but we managed. When we got to the Powell's we asked if we could leave the pram in the house, as it would not look good to have a pram in the car on the Glamis showfield! They laughed and wondered what two old guys like us needed a pram for. Bertie soon told them, "It's him you see, takes a lot of drink, then I have to wheel him round!"

After that we motored to the showfield where the Glamis Extravaganza car rally would be for the next two days. Quite a lot of cars were there already and Bertie checked in the Standard and got a number, all ready for next day. Then we went back to the B and B, and tea and biscuits. Breakfast was set for 9am.

We arrived at Glamis showfield about twenty past ten and the field was filling up fast, cars, vans, lorries, you name it, it was there. Motor bikes, push bikes, stationery engines, huge steam traction engines, tractors, it was truly amazing. It really had to be seen to be believed. There were stalls selling all sorts of things and some selling bits and pieces of old cars. Bertie had a look round and made some purchases. As it was raining a man with a stall selling umbrellas was doing a roaring trade. We had our lunch in Glamis Castle tearoom and very good mince and tatties it was too. We met George Kerr from Sandwick. One of the cars on show was a Model A Ford, 1928 or 29, two tone fawn. It belonged to Raymond and Sheila Macdonald from Rothes, who were friends of Bertie's. They, with their two boys, had a caravan at the showfield caravan site and we were invited there for tea. Soon the first day was over and it was back to the B and B for more tea and biscuits.

On Sunday we were at the showfield about 10.15am and got the car into her place. It was raining quite heavy so I got on my waterproofs and welly boots, the grass was long and wet, and furthermore there had been a herd of Highland cattle there! I walked and filmed, took photos, and met and had a chat with Graham Johnston. Graham asked if I had seen the boys with the motor bikes? I had not but met them soon after. Frank Johnson and Gordon Stark were doing a 2,000 mile run for charity, from North Unst to Land's End. With them as back up were Joe Gray, Geordie Jacobson and Robbie Burgess. When I saw them they had just finished a major repair on one of the bikes. They are great guys. It's amazing what they can do with old bikes and cars.

Once more we had lunch in Glamis Castle. After lunch there were still a lot of things to see, like the big steam traction engines and the fairground organ. There was always something going on in the showring, pipebands, clowns etc and they had a double ended Mini, which at the end of the act parted with a loud bang. Then there was a line up of tractors. I remarked to Bertie that a certain man in Brindister

The double ended Mini with two drivers. © W.S.

The Fordson truck at Glamis.   © *W.S.*

would have liked to have had that lot. Some of them could have done with attention. Then I spotted a Fordson lorry just like the one I learned to drive with. It had been partly rebuilt and it was spotless.

Soon the commentator was calling cars to circle the showring. The commentator was John Duncanson. As we were in the first group to be

Bertie couldn't resist a Clattering Brig cream cake.   © *W.S.*

called, off we went. We were the first car to circle the ring and did so on our own for about ten minutes. John Duncanson waved us over to speak. He and Bertie talked and John asked where we came from and where we had been. He was quite amazed to hear we had been at a car rally in Warwickshire. It was broadcast all over the field.

Later we went to Raymond and Sheila's caravan and had tea, a dram and chat. A Church of Scotland minister named

Brian, was with them and he was a classic car man as well. He was building up a Studbaker at home and it should be on the road now. Farewells were said and we set off back to the B and B.

On Monday, 10th July, it was a fine dry day for our run to Aberdeen and on to the ferry for Shetland. We decided to go over Cairn-Na-Mount and stopped at the Clattering Brig tearoom for some refreshments and relaxation. Then it was on to Banchory to visit another Shetlander, my sister in law, Myra Durno. We sat and yarned for a while then set off for Aberdeen and the P&O, where they said it could be a bad trip as the wind was increasing. When the *St Clair* left Aberdeen we had a light meal then wisely went to bed, with me in the top bunk of course! The trip north was not too bad, after all. The run down to Warwickshire, and back, was a fine experience and it was real motoring. It's said that the best part of a holiday is coming home, and I think we were both thinking along that lines on the drive from Lerwick.

We shake hands after a successful tour.   © *Mr Powell*